I0839362

Wilde Genealogy

European and Canadian Heritage

Back splash cover: *Grain Elevator at La Salle Manitoba* 1931 by Walter J. Phillips. Library and Archives Canada, Acc. No. 1989-228-1 and C- 110906

Back image: Coat of Arms Galicia and Lodomeria, Austrian Empire and Austro-Hungarian Empire, 1772-1918

Available to print in the United States of America and Canada

ISBN 978-1986355926

Wilde Genealogy

European and Canadian Heritage

1800 - 1945

Kathleen Wilde

Author's Note

This book uses the original "Wild" surname for the 19th century European family history. It wasn't until later, in the early 20th century, that Mary Ann MacDonald Wild, living in Saskatchewan, changed the family surname to "Wilde" which subsequent generations now follow.

Table of Contents

Foreword

I was fortunate to hear firsthand from Aunt Kay the emigration and pioneering stories she experienced and heard from her parents and grandparents. Aunt Kay has documented the Wilde family history for many years. She kept scrupulous notes, maps, family group documents and genealogy charts. After sharing her notes and an extensive array of family photos from her private collection, we came to the conclusion that a permanent record of this wonderful content was needed.

Aunt Kay's ability to capture word of mouth story-lines has put her in a unique position. Aunt Kay witnessed the pioneering lifestyle in a small village in the Prairie Provinces of Canada. Her knowledge base goes back 150 years from stories of our ancestors from Austria, Scotland and the Maritime province of Nova Scotia.

Being the oldest in a family of four brothers, Aunt Kay guided her brothers in their formative years. Her pioneer father, Thomas Wild, although not formally educated, took great pride in seeing his sons and daughter graduate from college.

Aunt Kay has been a lifetime promoter of Canada. With a career at Air Canada, she has travelled the world many times over, before settling in St. Bruno, Quebec caring for her parents. Currently, she resides in Niagara Falls, Ontario.

Aunt Kay loves Canada, loves her relatives and is the true Canadian in our family.

Brian Wilde
Philadelphia, Pennsylvania
March 23, 2018

Introduction

The reason I created this book was to allow future generations to understand where they are from and the situations our forefathers endured, both living in Europe, Nova Scotia and settling in the Canadian Prairie Provinces. The second reason is for those interested in our immigration path to Canada and our travels within Canada.

Much of the information came directly from conversation with my parents and grandparents. For this I am grateful for the opportunity to share with others.

Kathleen Wilde
Niagara Falls, Ontario
March 23, 2018

"Think... of the world you carry within you."

Rainer Maria Rilke
Austrian Poet

"We two have paddled in the stream,
from morning sun till dine;
But seas between us broad have roared
since auld lang syne (long long ago)."

Robert Burns
Scottish Poet

"Keep in mind that people change, but the past doesn't."

Becca Fitzpatrick
Author

Chapter 1. European Roots

The Wedding

It was the day before his marriage, February 15, 1886 and the twenty five year old Franz Wild was glad to be back home, having completed three years of compulsory military service in the Austrian-Hungarian army.[1] He had travelled to Vienna, Austria for training and had been on active duty in several nearby towns including Grodek and the nearby larger city of Lemberg. Franz was now a military reservist and could settle down and get married. In addition to several of his close military friends who travelled by horse and carriage, his large extended family were excited about the wedding, including his six brothers and sisters and their families.

Franz could be considered a middle child. He had two older brothers; Johann and Josef. Johann died at a young age. Joseph, also served his mandatory time in the military. Franz had two older sisters, Anna and Katharina; and two younger sisters, Apolonia and Eva. Franz had one younger brother named Thomas.

Franz married Veronica Kleczko whom he had known in his village since they were young. Veronica was 18 years old and lived in house 154. Franz lived in house 116 with his family and when not performing reserve military duties was a farmer and a carpenter. He worked on tables and chairs and the building of houses when not farming.

Franz Wild's Birth

Franz was born Franciscus Wild or Franz Wild in German in the small village of Muzylowice, Austro-Hungarian Empire on May 10, 1861. He was baptized on May 11, 1861.[2]

Franz's father was Johann Wild and his mother was Apolonia, daughter of Johann Schnerch and Veronica nee Jestadt, both German colonists. Godparents for the baptism were Franz Schnerch, colonist, and Catharina Wittman, unmarried.

Auxiliary godparents were Johann Schnerch, colonist, and Katharina, wife of Martin Hutter, colonist.[3] Second set of auxiliary godparents were Joseph Wild and Apolonia Schnerch, unmarried.

Franz was named after his godfather, Franz Schnerch.[4]

Veronica Kleczko's Birth

Veronica Kleczko, house 154, was born on July 2nd, 1868 and baptized on the same day. Veronica's father was Johann Kleczko, colonist. Veronica's mother was Maria, the daughter of Josef Sznerch (sic Schnerch) and Jakobina Jestadt. Godparents were Conrad Jestadt, colonist and Anna Lautsch, unmarried at the time.[5]

The child was baptised by Rev. Kazimierz Adamowski and the midwife was Victoria Magnowska.[6] Veronica's grandmother was Jakobina Jestadt.

The name Sznerch is the Polish phonetic spelling of the correct German surname Schnerch.[7]

More on the Wedding

At the time of the wedding, Franz Wild was living in house 116 in Muzylowice, 25 years of age, and son of Johann Wild and Apolonia Schnerch, colonists. Veronica Kleczko, was living in house 154, 18 years of age, and the daughter of Johann Kleczko and Maria Schnerch, both lifelong residents of Muzylowice.[8] So Franz was seven years older than Veronica.

The witnesses to the marriage were Mathias Gross and Thomas Kornel. Thomas was Franz's brother-in-law as he was the husband of Katharina Wild.[9]

Franz was only three years old when his oldest brother Johann Wild, born in house 116 on April 10, 1850, had passed away from an inflammation of the lungs. He was named after his godfather, Johann Schnerch and had lived to fifteen years of age.[10]

Most likely all the brothers and sisters of Franz Wild attended the wedding to Veronica Kleczko on February 16, 1886. They had several things in common, one; they were all born in the same house, 116, and second; most were named after their godparent, as was the Catholic German custom of the time. Here are their ages, marital status and family at the time of his wedding:

• Josef Wild, age 33, born December 13, 1852. He was named after his godfather, Josef Schnerch. Josef was married to Marianna *Lenius* and had five children, including an infant at the time of the wedding.[11]

• Anna Elizabeth Wild Kornel, age 29, born Jan 27, 1856, named after her godmother, Elizabeth Schnerch. Elizabeth Wild was married to Anton *Kornel,* brother to Thomas and had eight children between 1876-1890. Three living children could have attended the wedding with their parents.[12]

• Katharina Wild Kornel, age 27, born Jan 24, 1859, named after her godmother Katharina Ziegler. She was married to Thomas *Kornel.* They had six children, including an infant at the time of the wedding. Thomas was a witness to the marriage.[13]

• Franz Wild, age 25, born May 10, 1861.[14] The groom.

• Apolonia Wild Runge, age 22, born Nov 21 1863 and named after her mother.[15] Married to George *Runge.* They lived in the nearby hamlet of Czarnokonce that belonged to the Muzylowice Roman Catholic Parish. (The Runge family later immigrated to Canada.)

• Eva Wild, age 19, born Aug 30, 1866 named after her godmother, Eva Hillich.[16] Eva was not yet married at the time of the wedding. She later married Philip *Runge* the year following this wedding (m. 9-May-1887 in Münchenthal). (The family later immigrated to Canada.)

• Thomas Wild, age 17, born Jan 2, 1869 named after his godfather, Thomas Otto.[17] Thomas was not yet married at the time of the wedding. He married Eva *Wittmann* six years later. (m. 23-May-1892 in Münchenthal)[18]

It can be noted, that the second oldest boy of Johann and Apolonia Wild, Josef Wild was born on December 13, ironically the same birth day as the author of this book, Kathleen Wilde and the authors father, Thomas John Wild. The birth date of December 13 carries for three generations.

Also, the name Thomas carried for three generations; from Franz's brother *Thomas* Wild, to Franz's son *Thomas* John Wild, to Thomas John Wild's grandson, *Thomas* Gregory Wilde.

The Visitation of Our Blessed Mary Church in Muzylowice.[19] This is the church Franz and Veronica Wild were married. Also referred to as the Muzylowice Roman Catholic Parish.

Franz Wild in the uniform of Austro-Hungarian army.[20] Circa 1883.

The rank collar badge shows two six-point stars. This is an Austro-Hungarian officer's rank of "Oberleutnat" or "Korporal". This is the equivalent rank of Corporal in The Canadian Forces.[21]

Common Austro-Hungarian Badges of Rank.[22] Franz was a Corporal, attending the Vienna Military Academy in Vienna, Austria.

Franz's father was *Johann Baptist Wild*. Johann was born in house 109 (see Münchenthal map) on June 26, 1830 and baptized on the same day. Johann Baptist was the son of Johann Wild, who was a shoemaker in the village and Christina, the daughter of Phillip Zapf. Godparents were Anzelmus Huferek and Barbara, the wife of Michael Gurski. The child was baptized by Fr. Thomas Domaradzki and the midwife was Elizabeth Haas.

Johann was named after St. John the Baptist whose feast day is June 24th, two days before Johann's birthday. The feast day or name day is often celebrated instead of the actual birthday.

Saint John the Baptist icon by the Monks of Tabor.[23]
Johann Wild was named after the saint.

The feast day of Saint John the Baptist was a very popular event in the Ancien Régime of France. It also became known as Saint-Jean-Baptiste Day in Quebec, Canada.

The Roman Catholic Church

The physical church building of the Muzylowice Roman Catholic Parish was built in 1849 using bricks from the former adjacent Jesuit monastery that was closed by Emperor Josef II. This freed up tracts of lands where German colonists were settled.[24] The Wild's were parishioners of this Church. The church was also known as the Münchenthal Roman Catholic Parish.

The Wild's had extensive roots in the two small rural villages within Muzylowice with lineage going back for several generations.

The Muzylowice Roman Catholic Church and the priest in particular, played an important role in the lives of these German colonists, including the Wild's major life events. The parish priest was required to fully transcribe the parish registers each year and send copies to the Bishop's office.

Most of the parish records survived the wars that were to follow. The original transcripts sent to the Bishop were hand copied, much like the parish register itself. Therefore, through the generations, the church records have remained relatively intact and a source of valuable information. Original parish register books of birth, marriage and death are held by the Archive of Old Documents (AGAD) in Warsaw, Poland.[25]

Names in the Roman Catholic Church

Austrian law dictated that given names in the parish registers had to be rendered in Latin. So, for Franz Wild, Franciscus is the Latin version of his name, and Franz would be the German name. But in normal usage people would use the version of the name for the language they spoke.

> "So taking John as an example …. the parish or vital records would have Joannes (Latin) but if the person were German speaking he would use Johann, or if he was Polish speaking it would be Jan, or Ukrainian would be Ivan (pronounced as "ee-von").
>
> I am assuming that Veronica's father would use the Polish version of the name John, not the German name Johann or the Latin Joannes as given in the record. But we can't be certain in many

cases. Usually the Germans used German names, but some of the Germans used the Polish first name and usually the Poles used Polish first names, but some of the Poles used German first names.

But one thing for sure, is that from this time to the end of the colony, the priest would always use the Polish name wherever he could. The Polonization of the German colonists was a big point of contention between them and the priest. There is a whole history lesson to be told about this in the village. The priest used Latin in these records because the Austrian Monarchy decreed in 1784 exactly how the metrical records of birth, marriage and death were to be kept and one of the requirements was that Latin was the language to be used in the records."[26]
- Brian J. Lenius

Austrian History

Franz Wild (1861-1892), his wife and sons lived in the Galicia province of Austria-Hungary often referred to as the Austro-Hungarian Empire, ruled by Emperor Franz Josef in the last half of the 19th century (1848-1916). During this period Austria comprised a vast area and was not the small country it is today.

Austro-Hungarian Empire with Galicia province.[27]

It was a joint ruling of two nations: Austria and Hungary ruled by the Hapsburg Monarchy. The Austrian Empire extracted from Galicia considerable wealth and conscripted large numbers of the peasant population into its armed services. The Austro-Hungarian Empire ruled from 1867 to 1918, when at the end of the first world war, the Empire collapsed.

Franz Josef I ca.1885. [28]

During Franz Josef's reign Austria was the home of many scientists and world famous musicians, like Johannes Brahms, the symphony conductor. Vienna was then and still is the "city of music". Franz Joseph was a man of peace and was well loved by his people. The Habsburg bureaucracy is generally considered to be strict but honest and very well-organized.

Coat of Arms of Galicia and Lodomeria. The three crowns below the Jackdaw bird represent Galicia and Lodomeria and Bukovina.[29]

Former Austro-Hungarian province of Galicia is shown in red stripes located between todays Poland and Ukraine.[30]

The Village With Three Generations of Wilds

Muzylowice, phonically pronounced, "Mousiwoveetza", is also known as the German village of Münchenthal, (pronounced "Moonshental") established in 1783. It is currently known as Muzhylovychi, Ukraine.

There were two villages named Muzylowice: Muzylowice Narodowe and Muzylowice Kolonia. A villager could easily walk along the roads from one village to the other and not realize they had crossed from one to the other. Muzylowice was a German settlement where Franz and Veronica Wild were born and lived their married life. The village of Muzylowice was home to three generations of Wild and Kleczko families.

Muzylowice Narodowe is a polish village name. The "Narodowe" name literally means "national". The "Kolonia" name means "colony". As Brian J. Lenius further explains:

> "So to distinguish the two communities, one was called the colony and the other was called the "national" or "native" village. Often they simply referred to it as the "Ukrainian village" as opposed to the German colony. And some of the German families lived in the Ukrainian village, the Wild and Lenius families included."

Map of the German colonies in Galicia, province in the Austro-Hungarian Empire as of 1939.[31] The solid black circle east of Lemberg is the German Catholic village called Munchenthal on the map. Also known as Muzylowice.

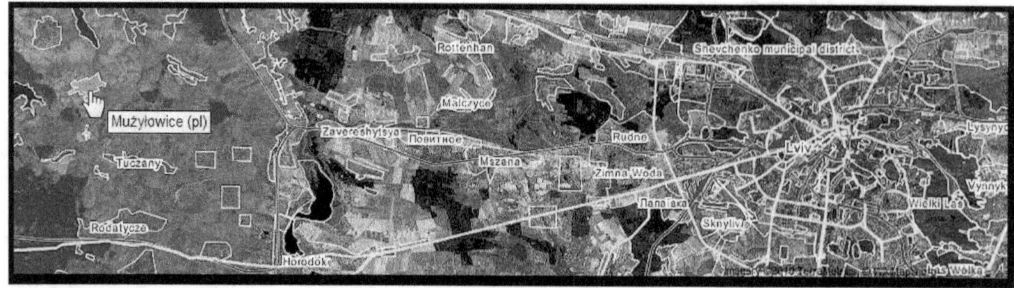

Current day map showing Muzylowice village on the left. The larger city on the right is the current day L'viv Ukraine.[32]

Muzylowice Village Details

"Muzylowice Kolonia had 188 females and 217 males for a total of 405 people. Muzylowice Narodowe had 580 females and 536 males for a total of 1,116 people. In the year 1900 there were only 74 houses in the German colony but there were 192 in the Ukrainian community. Most of the colony were composed of Germans."[33]

Muzylowice map 1869-1887.[34]

Franz Wild could have easily walked down the street to visit his siblings and the Schnerch in-laws. In most cases, the house owner also owned small parcels of land for growing crops. These parcels would be scattered around the periphery of the community borders. Unlike houses in rural Canada and the USA, the farmers houses were all together in a village cluster with the land parcels in an outer ring around the village.

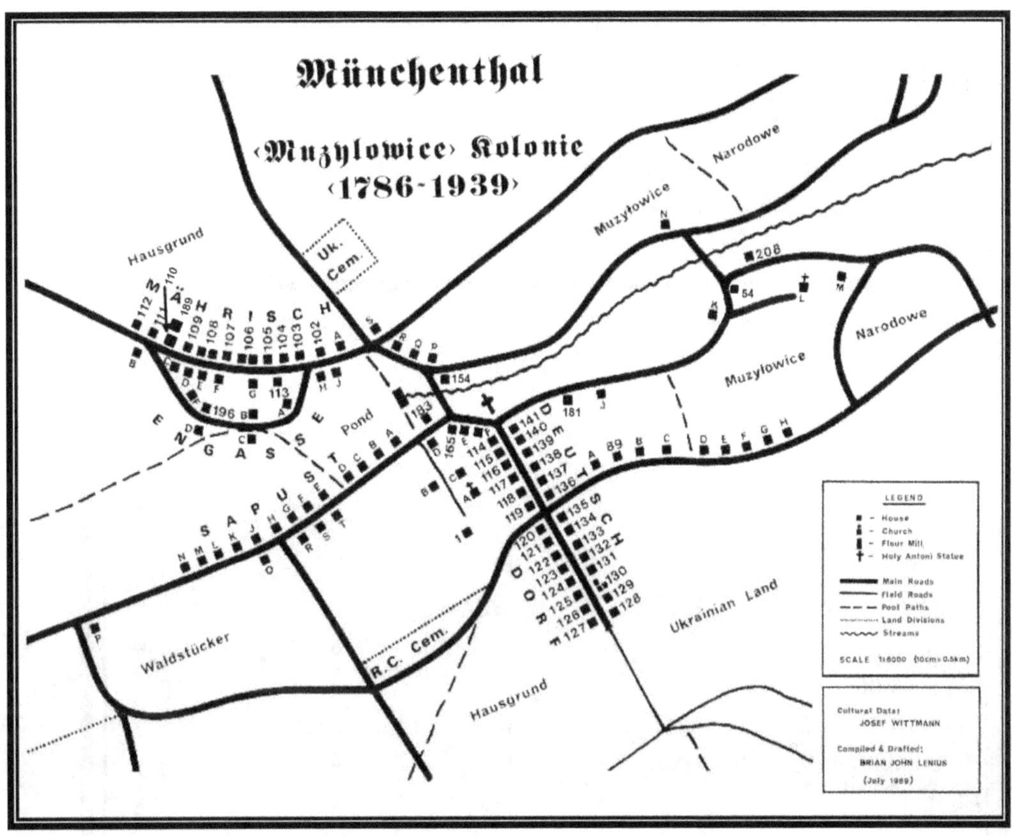

Map showing Muzylowice Kolonia (German colony) and Muzylowice Narodowe (Ukrainian community) ca. 1925. Generally, the numbers lower than 100 are in the Ukrainian village, from 100 to 141 were in the German colony, and higher numbers were both.[35]

The two Muzylowice communities had equal status during the Austrian Empire. Muzylowice Narodowe was primarily made up of Ukrainian families, while Muzylowice Kolonia, the German colony, was primarily German. However, there were a few German families in the Ukrainian village and a few Ukrainians in the German village. There were only a few families of Poles and they were in both villages.[36]

The family's house number is how the Roman Catholic Church followed its parishioners. Veronica Kleczko was born and lived in house 154. Franz Wild was born and lived in house 116 with his siblings. Franz and Veronica married and lived in house 181 where they had their sons. Franz died in house 189.

MÜNCHENTHAL CATHOLIC CEMETERY BURIALS
1787 – 1905

SURNAME	FIRST BURIAL	LAST BURIAL	NUMBER	% of Total
Schnerch	1794	1902	148	9.37%
Jost	1787	1896	118	7.47%
Schönhofer	1792	1896	110	6.97%
Jestadt	1796	1900	89	5.64%
Lautsch	1792	1902	86	5.45%
Wittmann	1792	1898	57	3.61%
Rostek	1792	1900	51	3.23%
Braumberger	1796	1902	45	2.85%
Gabel	1795	1896	44	2.79%
Wild	1834	1895	42	2.66%
Otto	1796	1902	41	2.60%
Massinger	1787	1902	38	2.41%
Weiss	1800	1902	34	2.15%

The Wild family in the Munchenthal Roman Catholic Cemetery.[37] There were forty two Wild family members buried in this cemetery between 1834 and 1895.

The New Family

These are the children of the Franz and Veronica Wild family:

• The first child *Karl (Carolus) Wild.* The first child of Franz and Veronica was Karl (Carolus) Wild, born Jan 9, 1888 and baptised Jan 15, 1888. At this time Johann Wild had passed away, but Apolonia was there to witness her son Franz and daughter-in-law Veronica's first child. The Godparents were Karl Wild, a colonist and Rosalia, wife of Johann Höhn, also a colonist. The child was baptised by Rev. Jan Urbanczyk and the midwife was Victoria Wittmann. The infant Karl Wild was named after his godfather Karl Wild.[38]

• Tragedy strikes the family. At 14 days old, infant Karl died, the cause of death was "debility". This shocked the new family although infant deaths at the time were astoundingly high. For this time in the late 19th century, infant mortality in NYC was at 20 percent, that is the child never reached their first birthday and 18 percent died before the age of five. They typically died of pneumonia, diphtheria and gastroenteritis.[39]

• The second child was *Thomas Wild*, house 181, born Dec 13, 1888, and baptised Dec 17, 1888. Thomas would become one of the patriarchs of the Wild family. As mentioned, Thomas' father was Franz Wild, son of Johann Wild (deceased) and Apolonia, born Schnerch, farmer. Thomas' mother was Veronica Kleczko, daughter of Johann Kleczko and Marianna born Schönhofer [sic Schnerch]. Godparents were Heinrich Jost, farmer and Eva Jost, unmarried daughter of Heinrich. The child was baptised by Rev. Jan Urbańczyk and the midwife was Victoria Wittmann.[40]

• Midwifes, like Victoria Wittmann, were common in this era as births in the rural areas were at home, not in a hospital. The nearest hospital was probably a half day away by horse and carriage in Lemberg.

• Their next child was born on February 24, 1891 and named *Karl (Carolus) Wild*, after his deceased little brother Karl, as was the common practice of the time. Godparents were Philip Runge, farmer in Weissenberg and Katharina, wife of Thomas Kornel. The child was baptised by Rev. Michael Beister and the midwife was Victoria Wittmann.[41]

• *Stanislaus Wild* was born on July 17, 1893. Godparents were Johann Kleczko, shoemaker, and Anna, wife of Heinrich Gross. The child was baptised by Rev. Michael Beister and the midwife was Victoria Wittmann.[42]

Note that there were no middle names given at the time of birth for the the Wild children, as evidence of the birth records. Later in life, Veronica and two of the boys acquired a middle name. Veronica's middle name became Ethel; *Veronica Ethel Wild*, Thomas's middle name became John; *Thomas John Wild*, Stanislaus middle name became Aloysius; *Stanley Aloysius Wild*. Karl never received a middle name, although his first name became "Carl"; *Carl Wild*. Ironically, the author Kathleen Wilde, daughter of Thomas John Wild, has no middle name. More on the addition of the "e" to the surname "Wild" later in this book.

Lineage Charts of the Wild Family

The following lineage charts outline the Franz Wild and Veronica Kleczko ancestry; including children, siblings, parents and grandparents. The last chart is the lineage of Thomas John Wild.[43]

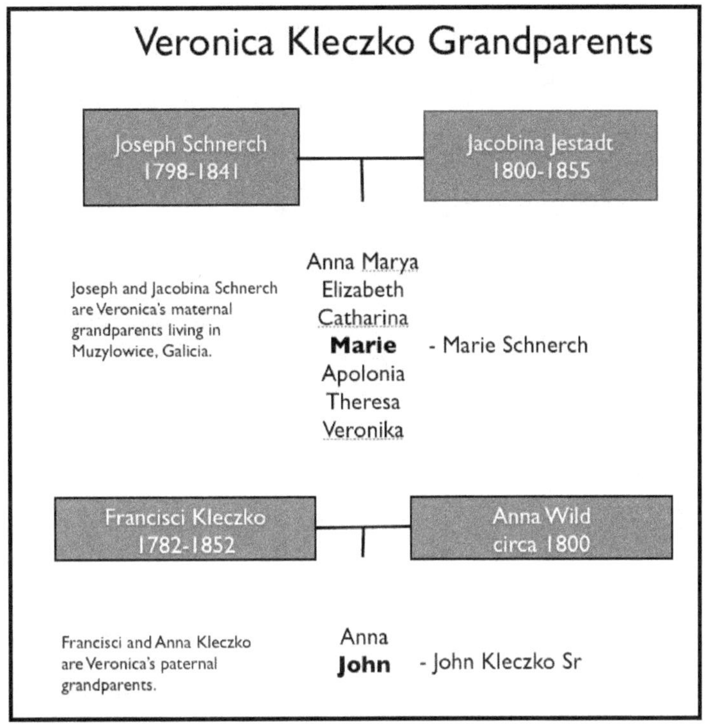

Veronica Kleczko Grandparents

Joseph Schnerch
1798-1841

Jacobina Jestadt
1800-1855

Joseph and Jacobina Schnerch are Veronica's maternal grandparents living in Muzylowice, Galicia.

Anna Marya
Elizabeth
Catharina
Marie   - Marie Schnerch
Apolonia
Theresa
Veronika

Francisci Kleczko
1782-1852

Anna Wild
circa 1800

Francisci and Anna Kleczko are Veronica's paternal grandparents.

Anna
John   - John Kleczko Sr

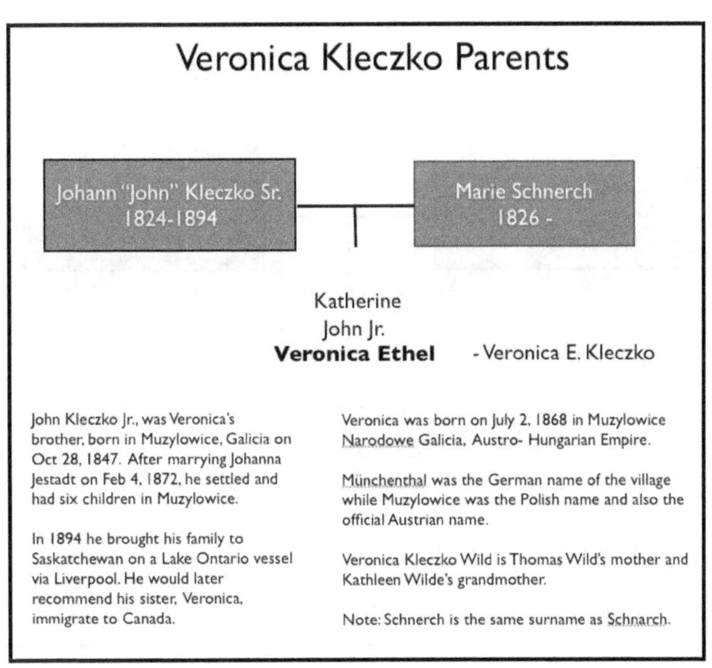

Veronica Kleczko Parents

Johann "John" Kleczko Sr.
1824-1894

Marie Schnerch
1826 -

Katherine
John Jr.
Veronica Ethel   - Veronica E. Kleczko

John Kleczko Jr., was Veronica's brother, born in Muzylowice, Galicia on Oct 28, 1847. After marrying Johanna Jestadt on Feb 4, 1872, he settled and had six children in Muzylowice.

In 1894 he brought his family to Saskatchewan on a Lake Ontario vessel via Liverpool. He would later recommend his sister, Veronica, immigrate to Canada.

Veronica was born on July 2, 1868 in Muzylowice Narodowe Galicia, Austro- Hungarian Empire.

Münchenthal was the German name of the village while Muzylowice was the Polish name and also the official Austrian name.

Veronica Kleczko Wild is Thomas Wild's mother and Kathleen Wilde's grandmother.

Note: Schnerch is the same surname as Schnarch.

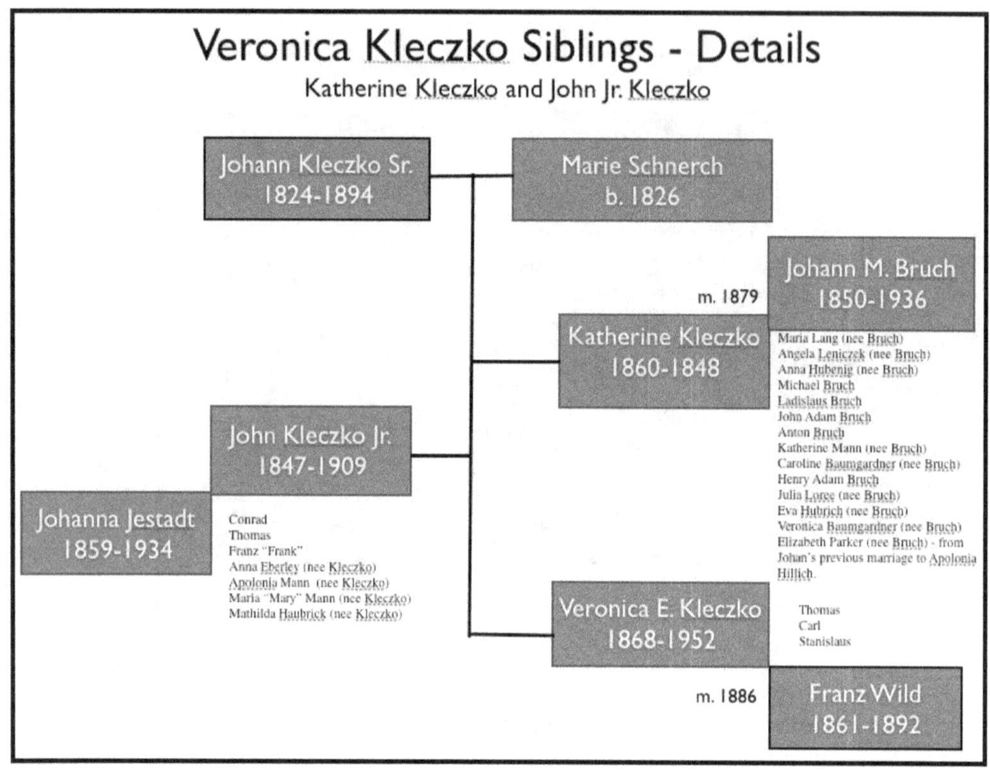

Veronica Kleczko Siblings - Details
Katherine Kleczko and John Jr. Kleczko

Johann Kleczko Sr.
1824-1894

Marie Schnerch
b. 1826

m. 1879

Johann M. Bruch
1850-1936

Katherine Kleczko
1860-1848

Maria Lang (nee Bruch)
Angela Leniczek (nee Bruch)
Anna Hubenig (nee Bruch)
Michael Bruch
Ladislaus Bruch
John Adam Bruch
Anton Bruch
Katherine Mann (nee Bruch)
Caroline Baumgardner (nee Bruch)
Henry Adam Bruch
Julia Loree (nee Bruch)
Eva Hubrich (nee Bruch)
Veronica Baumgardner (nee Bruch)
Elizabeth Parker (nee Bruch) - from
Johan's previous marriage to Apolonia
Hillich.

John Kleczko Jr.
1847-1909

Conrad
Thomas
Franz "Frank"
Anna Eberley (nee Kleczko)
Apolonia Mann (nee Kleczko)
Maria "Mary" Mann (nee Kleczko)
Mathilda Haubrick (nee Kleczko)

Johanna Jestadt
1859-1934

Thomas
Carl
Stanislaus

Veronica E. Kleczko
1868-1952

m. 1886

Franz Wild
1861-1892

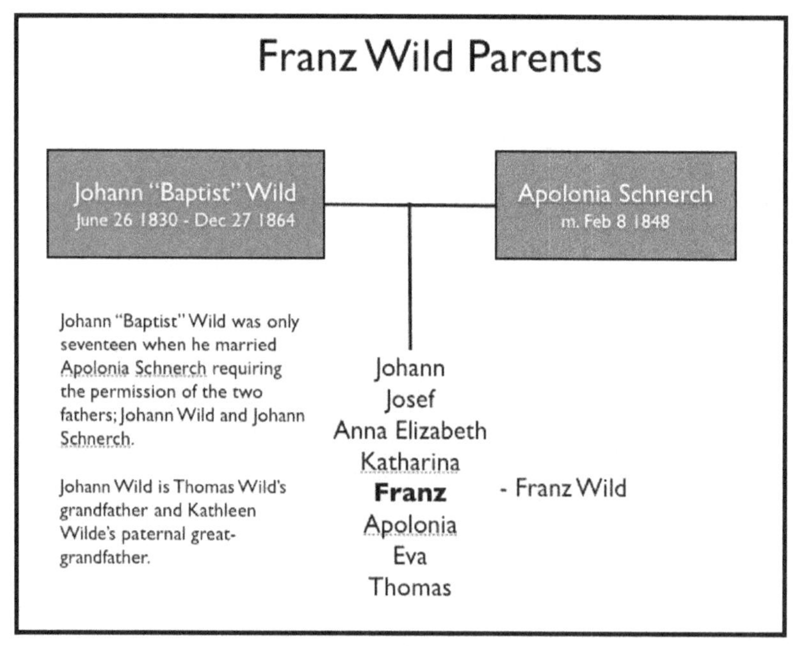

Franz Wild Parents

Johann "Baptist" Wild
June 26 1830 - Dec 27 1864

Apolonia Schnerch
m. Feb 8 1848

Johann "Baptist" Wild was only
seventeen when he married
Apolonia Schnerch requiring
the permission of the two
fathers; Johann Wild and Johann
Schnerch.

Johann Wild is Thomas Wild's
grandfather and Kathleen
Wilde's paternal great-
grandfather.

Johann
Josef
Anna Elizabeth
Katharina
Franz   - Franz Wild
Apolonia
Eva
Thomas

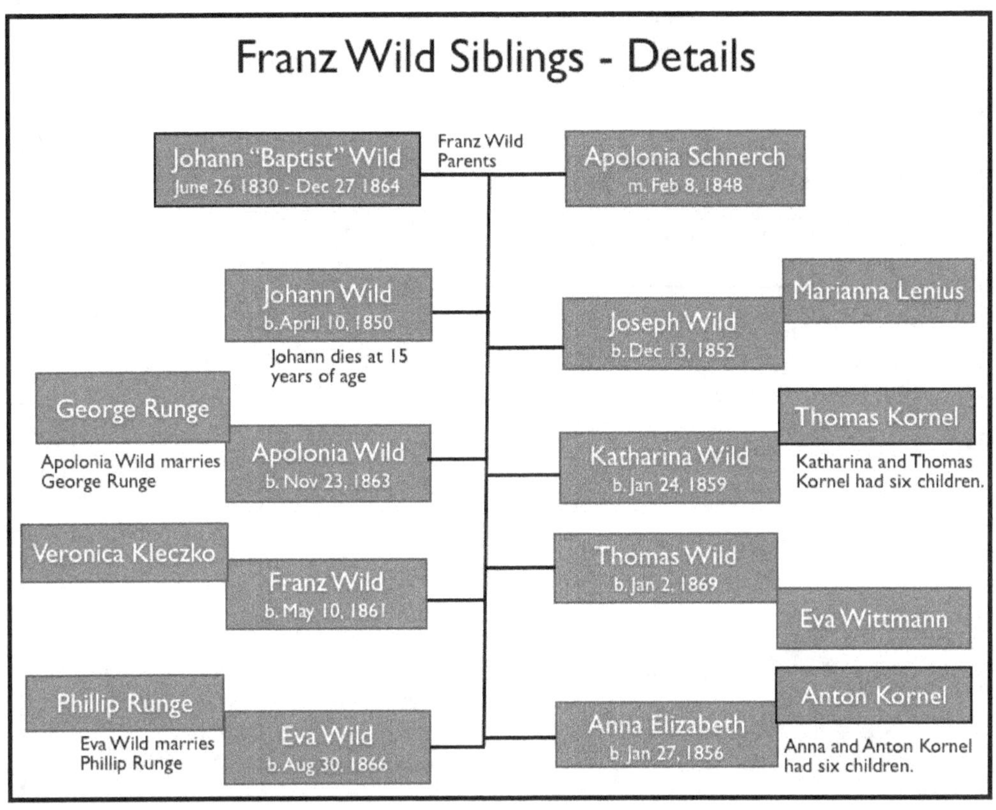

Franz Wild Siblings - Details
Franz Wild Parents
Johann "Baptist" Wild
June 26 1830 - Dec 27 1864
Apolonia Schnerch
m. Feb 8, 1848
Johann Wild
b. April 10, 1850
Johann dies at 15 years of age
Joseph Wild
b. Dec 13, 1852
Marianna Lenius
George Runge
Apolonia Wild marries George Runge
Apolonia Wild
b. Nov 23, 1863
Katharina Wild
b. Jan 24, 1859
Thomas Kornel
Katharina and Thomas Kornel had six children.
Veronica Kleczko
Franz Wild
b. May 10, 1861
Thomas Wild
b. Jan 2, 1869
Eva Wittmann
Phillip Runge
Eva Wild marries Phillip Runge
Eva Wild
b. Aug 30, 1866
Anna Elizabeth
b. Jan 27, 1856
Anton Kornel
Anna and Anton Kornel had six children.

Franz and Veronica Wild
and Frank and Veronica Golling

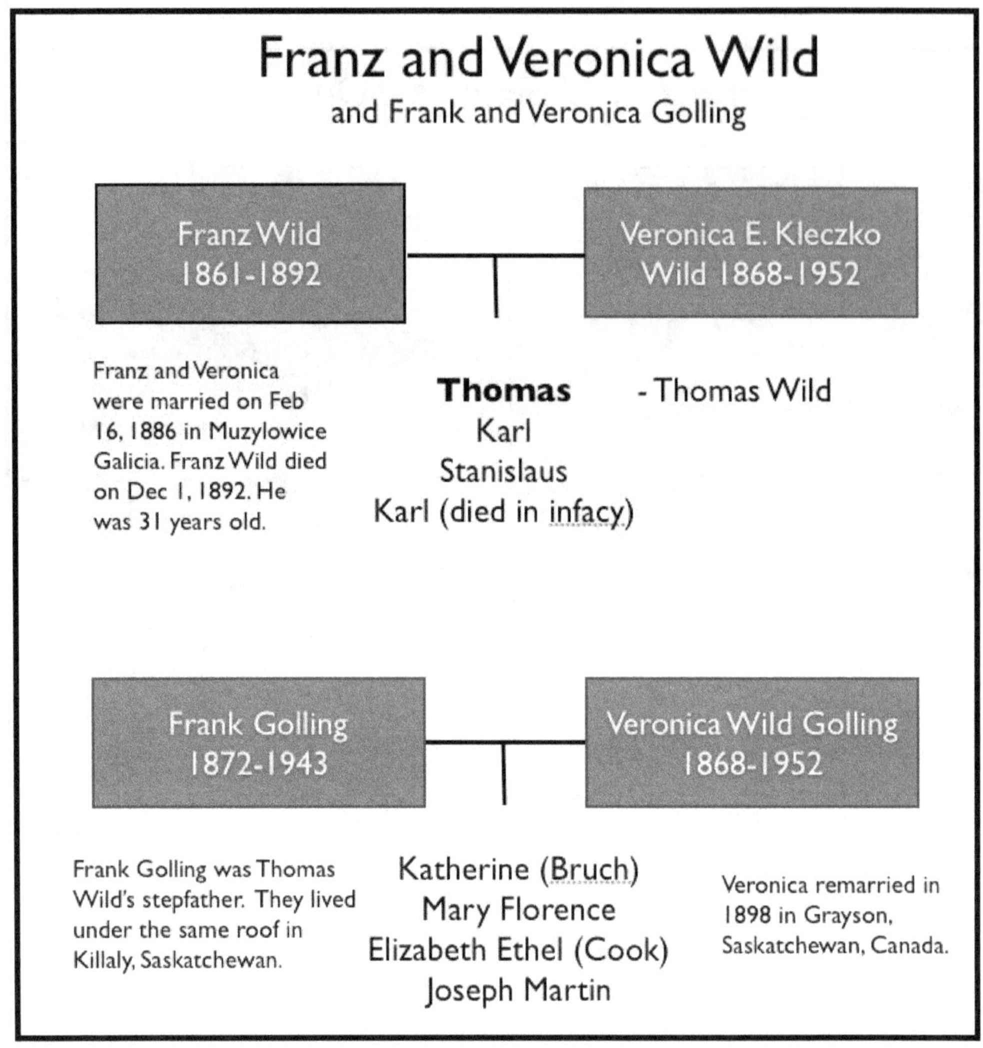

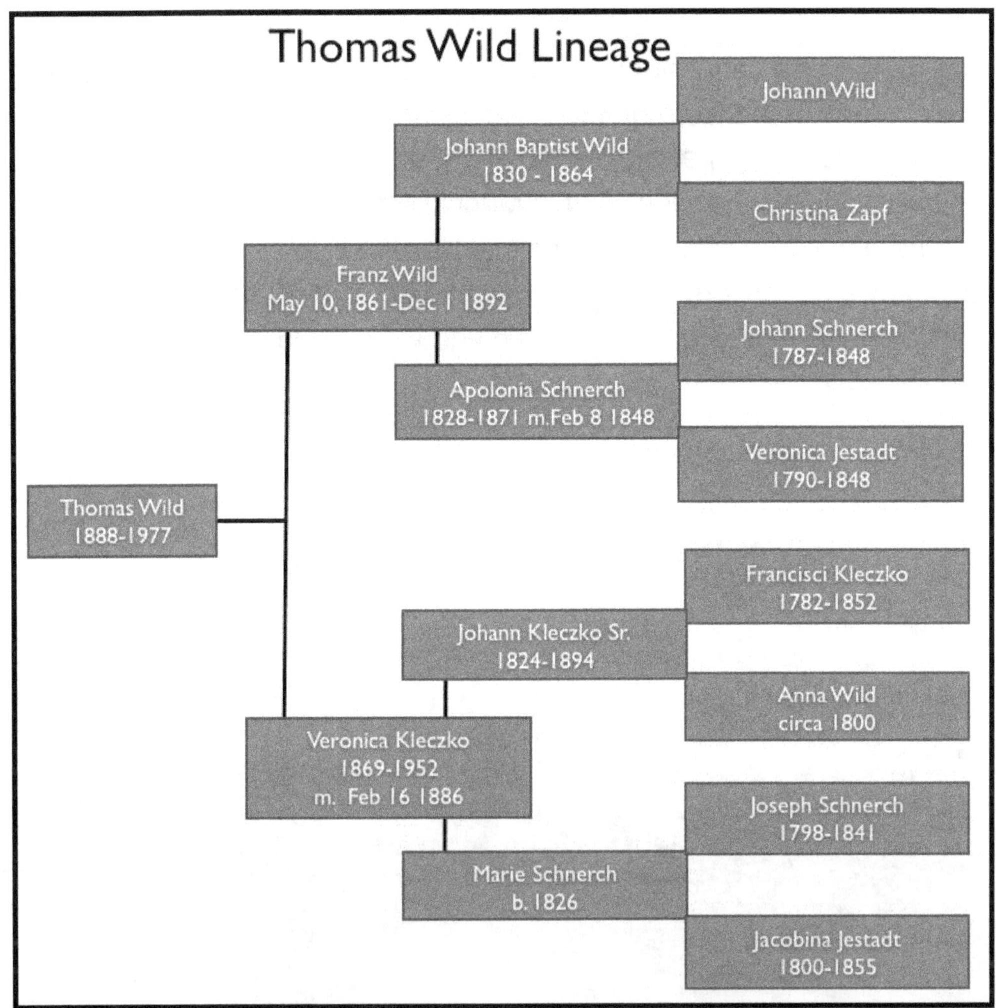
Thomas Wild Lineage
Johann Wild
Johann Baptist Wild
1830 - 1864
Christina Zapf
Franz Wild
May 10, 1861-Dec 1 1892
Johann Schnerch
1787-1848
Apolonia Schnerch
1828-1871 m.Feb 8 1848
Veronica Jestadt
1790-1848
Thomas Wild
1888-1977
Francisci Kleczko
1782-1852
Johann Kleczko Sr.
1824-1894
Anna Wild
circa 1800
Veronica Kleczko
1869-1952
m. Feb 16 1886
Joseph Schnerch
1798-1841
Marie Schnerch
b. 1826
Jacobina Jestadt
1800-1855

Village Commerce

Franz Wild was a carpenter by trade in addition to being a landowner and farmer. Many of the German men had a sideline occupation such as tailor, shoemaker, carpenter, or something else they could do out of their home in addition to farming. But in Münchenthal about the year 1925 there were at least seven Germans that were said to be shoemakers! How many shoemakers does a place with about 2,000 people need? So it was not a full time occupation as we know it although they may all have been skilled in the trade.

- Brian J. Lenius

Coin used in Franz Wild's time, an 1881 Gold 20 Franc from Austria-Hungary (1867-1918) with wreathed head of Franz Josef (l).[44] Crown of St. Saint Stephen on Hungarian royal arms (r), with 20 Franc and 8 Forint denomination.

A 20 Kronen banknote from the dual monarchy of Austria-Hungary.[45] In language of the Empire; Czech, Polish, Ruthenian (Ukrainian), Italian, Slovene, Croatian, Serbian, Romanian.

The note reads: The Austro-Hungarian bank shall, on demand, immediately pay for this banknote, at its head offices in Vienna and Budapest, *Twenty Crowns* in statutory metal coinage. The back side of the paper note is in Hungarian.

The Wilds in Muzylowice

The Wild family does not show up in the land records from 1820. So it was after that the Wild family first appeared in Muzylowice. The earliest known record to date for the Wild family in Muzylowice is the birth of Katharina Wild, daughter of Johann Wild and Christina Zapf on Nov 27, 1827. She is a sister to Johann Baptist Wild. The earliest Wild death record is from 1834 and earliest marriage is from 1830.[46]

The Military

After 1868, men were inducted into the military between the ages of 20 and 23. Active duty was for three years followed by nine years of Reserve duty.[47] This was a major deterrent for staying in the village for Veronica. She did not want her boys to be killed in action.

Defining Our German Colony

First of all we need to know the difference between a person's ethnicity and their nationality. The colonists were ethnically German, but they were citizens of the Austrian Empire (and after 1867 the Austro-Hungarian Empire). So their nationality was Austrian.

These newcomers were called colonists because the Austrian Monarchy in the 1780's embarked on a "colonization" program to bring people from Germany to the recently acquired land called Galicia (in German/Austrian it was called Galizien). This acquisition of territory was due to the partitioning of Poland in 1772. In 1772, without great warfare, the Austrian, Prussian, and Russian Empires basically divided the Polish Commonwealth among themselves. The part that Austria acquired was called Galicia (Galizien).

The area was already occupied for hundreds, if not thousands of years by Ukrainian and Polish peasants who most often were subservient (peasants) to the landlords or nobles. In some places there was no individual noble family. Instead there might be a religious order with a monastery. This was the case in Muzylowice. There was a Jesuit monastery there established in the 1600's when the landlord of the day passed his estate to the Jesuits. The land that these monasteries owned was basically the size of the large landlord holdings in other villages. As an aside, the church was built from bricks taken from the monastery buildings.

Emperor Josef II of Austria closed many monasteries in the 1780's because they were more about being land barons and less about religion. Even the Bernadine Monastery in Lemberg (now L'viv, Ukraine) was closed in 1784 and turned into an archive. That place has been a functioning archive ever since - more than 200 years. Today it is the Central State Historical Archive in L'viv and one of the oldest and largest archives in Europe.

Germans were invited by Josef II to come and settle on new land acquired from the religious orders in Galizien. The land in Muzylowice was from the recently closed Jesuit monastery. So these places became known as colonies and the people as colonists. One would think the label would only apply to the first generation, it was actually continued right until the end of the existence of the colonies during WWII. It was one way of distinguishing between the westerners (Germans speaking) and the nationals (Ukrainians and Poles).

So the term "German colonists" might be used because they were ethnically German (or German speakers) and were moved into this land (or their ancestors were). The colony is an island (of German language and culture) among a large area and overwhelming majority of another ethnicity (language, culture and religion) as in Ukrainians or Poles. A colony is typically located far away from the homeland of the people living there. We could use the term "Austrian colonies" when referring to any colonies in the Austrian Empire. For example, there were also Polish (ethnic) colonies in Galicia. They are usually settlements (like the German ones) as islands of Polish ethnicity in an otherwise Ukrainian area of native settlement usually to the east of the Polish homeland.[48]
- *Brian J. Lenius*

The Unsuspecting Illness

All was going well for Franz and Veronica until the spring of 1868 when Franz Wild contracted the deadly Typhus disease. Typhus was known to everyone in the Munchenthal community, including the Wild family, due to previous outbreaks.

Many typhus epidemics raged throughout Europe. In 1759, English authorities estimated about 25% of all prisoners in England died of Typhus. Between 1816 and 1819 over 100,000 Irish died from outbreaks of typhus. Typhus appeared again during the Great Irish Famine between 1846 and 1849. It killed people of all social classes, as lice were endemic and inescapable.

Typhus is a bacterial disease; there are two types termed endemic and epidemic. Endemic typhus are transmitted to humans by lice and fleas and can be spread where mice, rats and cats are in a high human population area.

Epidemic typhus, on the other hand, is a more severe typhus where a few animals like rats infect a large number of humans where poor and crowded living conditions exist. It is known as one of the great disease scourges in human history. Subjects have rash, sores and delirium.

Franz probably died from endemic form of typhus. The disease can occur any time of year, but many are infected during the spring or summer months when fleas and tics are most active. Franz Wild may have been infected in the winter months.

Endemic typhus develops one to two weeks after initial infection and includes a high fever (about 105 degrees) headache, nausea, vomiting and diarrhea. A rash on the chest or abdomen begins four days after initial symptoms. Symptoms last for about two weeks.

Modern medicine had not evolved yet. It wasn't until after 1909, when the French physician Charles-Jules-Henri Nicolle demonstrated that typhus is transmitted from person to person by the body louse. (Dr. Nicolle later won the Noble Prize for his efforts.) Alexander Fleming hadn't discovered penicillin until 1928. Today, antibiotics cure most people with typhus and would have surely cured Franz Wild.

Franz Wild who lived in House 189 with his family, died of Typhus on December 1, 1892. He was 31 years old, son of Johann Wild and married for seven years to Veronica (nee Kleczko) Wild.[49]

Franz was able to create a will for the boys, which would affect them in their adolescent years. The will stipulated the inherited funds from their father could not be used until their 18th birthday.

In the early 20th century typhus decreased and then practically disappeared from western Europe as improvements in living conditions and hygiene occurred.

Veronica is Surprised with a Third Boy

There were two boys in the family at the time of Franz's illness in 1891; Thomas was three years old and Karl was one year and 10 months old. Veronica was one month pregnant with the third boy when her husband Franz died. The third boy, Stanislaus, was not born until eight months after Franz's death, on July 17, 1893.

Veronica probably did not know she was pregnant until after Franz's death. Since Franz was ill for about two weeks (as was typical with typhus) before the illness took his life, he never knew his third boy, Stanislaus Wild.

Veronica Adapts Without a Husband

Veronica lived without a husband, was widowed and with three children for five years and that is a very long time in the colonies to be without a bread earner. Normally, when a father of a family dies it was absolutely necessary for the mother to remarry quickly in order to survive. Women in these times had no occupations except midwife and homemaker. They were responsible for the upbringing of their children. The same applied to men who were widowed. When the wife and mother died, he would have no means of taking care of his children or home. So often a widow/ widower would remarry within a short period of time, even as fast as six months. This was not considered wrong or disrespectful.[50]

Veronica considered Canada not knowing exactly what her future would bring, but assuming that it had to be better than her situation where she was living.

- Brian J. Lenius

The Canadian Government's Marketing Campaign

Veronica likely began noticing fliers marketing the Canadian West and heard from villagers and relatives who had already left for Canada. Veronica's sister Katherine Kleczko and her brother John Kleczko had already immigrated to Canada.

Fliers and posters were the technology of the day and the single most important of all visual marketing media. The Canadian government had a massive campaign circulating thousands of fliers to European cities.

A sample flier from Canada landing in Europe. The phrase, "The Last Best West" was used to advertise the Canadian West abroad.[51]

In addition to posters and fliers, pamphlets, with a long standing tradition of use in Western Europe dating back to the 15th century, were used. Between 1896 and 1913, the Canadian government produced hundreds of illustrated pamphlets in multiple languages for use by emigration agents, shipping lines, and government offices abroad to spark interest in moving to Canada.

Canada wanted the Prairie West to become its breadbasket to the world, linked by railways from the east coast. Wheat would flow south to the

USA. Yet to produce the wheat, Canada needed farmers to take root in the Prairie Provinces (Manitoba, Saskatchewan and Alberta).

Immigration to Canada often placed families from the same European area to the new towns in the Prairie provinces, so much so, the new towns were named after their European counterparts.[52]

A popular poster, Canada's Call to Women.[53]

In one such pamphlet mailing, in 1897, the year Veronica Wild emigrated, Canada's High Commissioner in London distributed a specially prepared pamphlet "through the post to every farmer in the United Kingdom, and to every blacksmith."[54]

In another distribution, pamphlets were sent to "the free libraries, reading rooms, farmers' and workmen's clubs and institutions, hotels, etc...." [55]

Advertising "free land" was a great incentive to "pull" potential immigrants into coming to Canada.[56] This poster in German: "160 Acres Frei, Westlichen Canada, fur jeden ansiedler" means "160 free acres in Western Canada for each settler".

Canada realized this media had great potential for creating a new image for the Prairie West. As the technology improved in the early years of the 20th century, the posters became more colorful and were simplified to carry less text. The images flaunted the fertility of the prairie land, with the season always summer and the fields always in crop or in the process of being harvested.

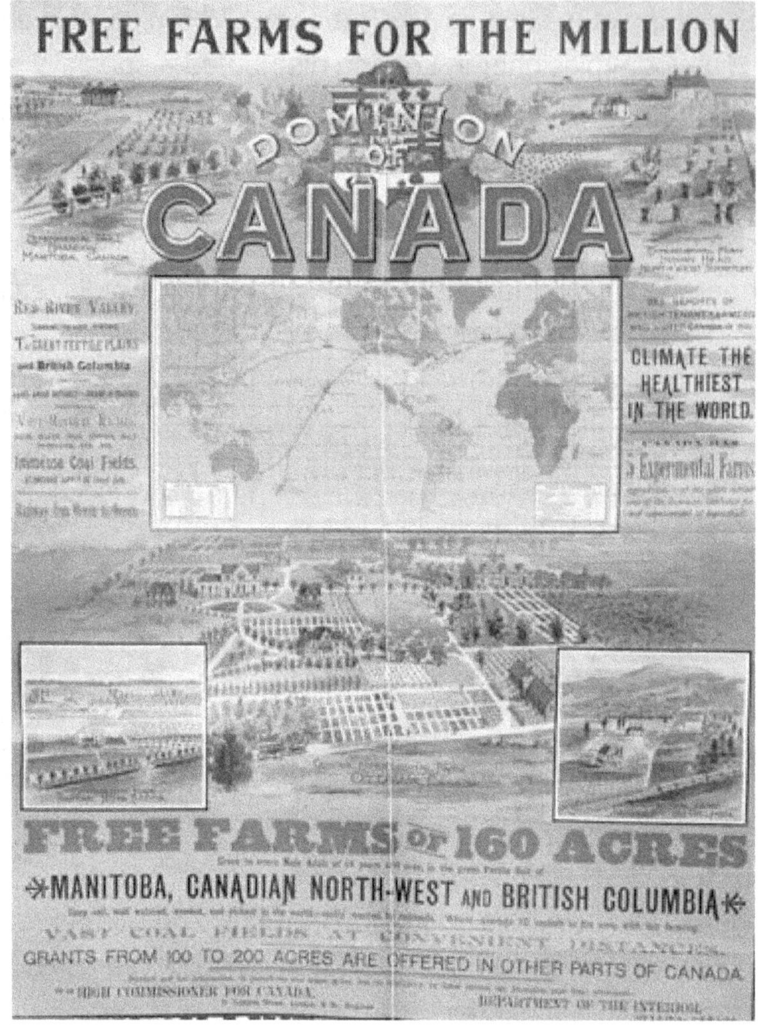

Canadian Department of Interior produced this poster using lithographic press allowing bright colors. Sample farms are in the inset. ca. 1893 [57]

When Clifford Sifton became Canada's Minister of the Interior in 1896, much of the Prairies had yet to be settled. Restrictive laws regulating the work of immigration agents forced Sifton to find more creative and clandestine methods of promoting Canada. He used an aggressive advertising policy aimed specifically at farmers from eastern Europe.[58]

Communications Between Continents

Communications between Veronica Wild in Austria and her sister Katherine Kleczko and brother John Kleczko in Canada were important to her after losing her husband Franz.

Letters would take several weeks or more from Europe to the Canadian midwest. Letters would leave Europe by steamship. In the 1880's within Canada, the Canadian Pacific Railway (C.P.R.) moved mail from the east coast to the Prairies. The postal system evolved alongside the railway system. The telegraph had been invented and was used domestically but it wasn't until later that the transatlantic telegraph became available between continents.

Typically, a Canada Post office was situated inside a general store or some other country business, such as a drug store or a private farm. Canada Post also had a bank service. Money orders could be sent through the Canada Post office.

The Boscurvis Saskatchewan Post Office (1897) was typical of early settlement times when someone's farm also served as the post office.[59]

The Kleczko's probably used the Canada Post office in a nearby rural town to send and receive letters with Veronica. The town of Neudorf, Saskatchewan situated 14 km west of Killaly, opened it's first Canada Post office in 1895. It was a divisional point or major intersection for the Canadian Pacific Railway (C.P.R.) and could have been used to pick up and send mail.[60]

It wasn't until 1908 that Rural Mail Delivery (RMD) brought the mail directly to the mail box of the post office's rural clientele along a main passage road. [61]

1897 Queen Victoria Diamond Jubilee Stamp. The left image is a painting of the young queen 1837, the right image a photo is her Diamond Jubilee photo from 1867. Between the portraits the initials VRI signify Victoria Queen and Empress. The Queen was monarch from 1837 until her death in 1901.[62]

Veronica Wild Decides to Leaves Europe

Veronica Wild decided to leave Europe and immigrate to Canada. There were a number of reasons why Veronica left the village of Muzylowice:

• Family in Canada played an important part in making the decision to immigrate and was likely an important one in Veronica's case as a widow.

• Veronica's older sister, Katherine came to Saskatchewan (even before John Kleczko) and may have influenced Veronica. They were one of the first families that settled in the area around Killaly, Saskatchewan called Mariahilf. Katherine and her husband Johan Michael Bruch along with their five children and her nephew Conrad Kleczko (son of Johann Kleczko) arrived in Canada about a year and a half before Johann Kleczko and family.[63]

• Veronica's brother, John Kleczko Jr., had moved to Canada and suggested she move to Lemberg, Saskatchewan. He offered to finance the trip.

• The marketing campaign by the Canadian government may have been an influence, promoting the positive aspects of the Prairie Provinces.

• Many immigrated to Canada to take advantage of the Dominions Land Act of 1872, a Canadian law that aimed at encouraging settlement of the Canadian Prairie Provinces. This law permitting settlers to acquire 160 acres to homestead and an additional 160 acres upon homesteading.

• With three young boys, the compulsory military training was a deterrent to staying.

- Johann Kleczko, Franz Golling Sr. and Franz Golling Jr. farmed near each other in Saskatchewan and attended the same church, so such discussions about a widow with three boys may have occurred.

- Possibly the Golling and Kleczko families may have been familiar with each other in Galicia as the Gollings emigrated from Wielopole (now Velykopole) 20 miles west of Muzylowice.

- Veronica lived in Muzylowice for five years as a widow with three children and possibly thought she had better chances of marrying in the West.

Further analysis by Brian J. Lenius:

> It is almost always a matter of "push and pull". One or more factors are pushing people to leave and one or more factors are pulling people to immigrate to the new land. If either is missing often people do not emigrate. People left the colonies due to hardship.

> Europe was overpopulated and there was little chance of increasing land holdings. Land was scarce even when the colonies were first established. The standard amount of land given to each colonist family was about 10-20 hectares (25 to 50 acres). There was no place for new generations to go other than inherit the family farm or marry someone who had inherited a family farm. As mentioned, the Canadian government was offering 160 acres free simply if the newcomer worked the land. And another 160 acres was possible for a very small fee after a few years. It was like a dream. Only the land barons or nobles could possibly dream of 320 acres of land in Europe.[64]

Travel Documents - Veronica Prepares to Leave

Passports were required, but not everyone had them and some "snuck out" of the country. Yet, a woman with three children would not likely do that. There were shipping line agents that visited individual villages in Europe including Galicia and almost certainly Muzylowice. They would extol the benefits of immigrating to Canada and probably often exaggerated it as they were paid a commission for each person that immigrated to Canada. Having said that, I don't think the agents accompanied the immigrants. Immigrants were expected to make their own way to the port city.

On the Hamburg-Amerika passenger list for this sailing there were two other families also from Muzylowice; Bula and Gilewicz. Some of the Gilewicz families were Roman Catholic and some were Greek Catholic, but the Bula family were strictly Greek Catholic. Veronica and her children most likely travelled with these two families, one of which was also a woman with children.

- Brian J. Lenius

Crossing the Atlantic: The Hamburg-Amerika Line

From 1881 until 1914, the Hamburg-Amerika Line was the largest shipping line in existence. The German city of Hamburg lies on the Elbe River, a navigable waterway that empties into the North Sea. It became the most important emigration port in continental Europe during the last decades of the nineteenth century.

German advertisement for the Hamburg-Amerika Line. The Wild family spoke and read German.[65]

As the flow of emigrants needing accommodation began to overwhelm the capacity of Hamburg's hotels and hostels, the government constructed an emigrant village, the Auswandererhallen (emigrant halls), built on Veddel Island in the Elbe, on the outskirts of Hamburg. It is possible that Veronica Wild and her three boys stayed overnight in this emigrant village.

Able to accommodate as many as five thousand people at one time, the village provided dormitories, kosher and non-kosher dining halls, shops, a bandstand, and houses of worship, including a synagogue.

It also had facilities for quarantine and further health inspections. When sailing day arrived, the passengers loaded their belongings onto tenders, which transported them down the Elbe to Cuxhaven, the city's deep-water outport, where the giant transatlantic ships awaited their boarding.

The steamship, which appeared in the 1850s, was the new means of crossing the Atlantic compared to the traditional sailing ship of the day. By 1867, over 80 percent of immigrants arrived in Canada by steamer. Prior to that, crossing the North Atlantic was a treacherous and life threatening passage and took several months.

The SS Arcadia Steamship is the ship Veronica and her sons travelled to Canada.[66]

The S.S. Arcadia ship of the Hamburg-Amerika Line was ready to set sail for Canada on April 10, 1897. Veronica E. Kleczko Wild (1869-1952) boarded the ship with her three young sons; Thomas John Wild (1888-1977), Carl Wild (1891-1971), and Stanislaus Aloysius Wild (1893-1975). All were born in Galicia, Austro-Hungarian Empire, were of the Roman Catholic faith and spoke German.

To this lady, Veronica Ethel Wild, we owe a great deal. She commenced her journey from Linz, Austria to the port in Hamburg, Germany. Travel from her home to the port of departure was in a cattle train.

The S.S. Arcadia maiden voyage with Captain H. Martens was as follows: departed Hamburg, Germany on April 10, 1897 to Antwerp, Belgium on April 16, 1897 and arriving in Montreal, Quebec on May 2, 1897. They encountered a storm en-route. The voyage took three weeks.[67]

The family travelled steerage class on the S.S. Arcadia, the part of the passenger ship allotted to passengers paying the lowest fare on the boat. Veronica recalled this as the lowest deck on the ship and witnessed her meager belongings thrown down. However, they were fed on the ship. The cost of a typical adult steerage ticket of 700 Kronos was equivalent to about twenty U.S. dollars or $555 in todays value. Children over five years of age were the same as adult fares.[68]

They travelled overland from Montreal, Quebec to Winnipeg, Manitoba and on to Lemberg, Saskatchewan.

Emigrants boarding a ship at the port of Hamburg.[69]

An Account of the 1897 Voyage of the Arcadia

The *1897 Voyage of the Arcadia* is a first hand account of crossing the Atlantic on the S.S. Arcadia by Dmytro Romanchych, who was on the same voyage as Veronica and her three young boys.

Dmytro Romanchych describes in detail the voyage including:

- sleeping on the lower decks packed on iron bedsteads
- high humid and resulting body stench
- took 21 days to get to from Hamburg, Germany to Montreal, Quebec
- hurricane weather and a "deluge of rain"
- many became seasick, two persons died; an old man and a child.
- stuck in an ice storm for three days.

Dmytro Romanchych account of the voyage is taken from *Early Ukrainian Settlements in Canada 1895-1900* by Vladimir J. Kaye. (University of Toronto Press, 1964):

> After a short wait in Hamburg, one and a half thousand Ukrainian emigrants were loaded into an very old but not very large ship, the Arcadia. It was a boat that had steam engines as well as sails which were hoisted when a favourable wind was blowing. Under the top deck there were about a dozen passenger cabins where the "city-coated gentlemen" travelled. Under the second deck were the galleys and the dining room. Below water level, under the third and fourth decks, there were no cabins, only one big space with rows of iron bedsteads, three or four stories high. In the lower beds the women and children slept, and in the upper beds, the men and boys. If one wished to reach the upper story, an iron ladder had to be used.
>
> We stopped over at Antwerp, in Belgium, where the boat took on ballast, hundreds of barrels with cement. We stayed at Antwerp for five days. Nobody was permitted to leave the boat, and only Budrug and Negrych [Iwan Bodrug and Iwan Negrych, both teachers] managed somehow to get off the boat and view the city. On the boat it was unbearably hot, and below deck an unbearable stench made breathing difficult.
>
> Probably no Ukrainian emigrant ever experienced such a dreadful ocean crossing as we did on our Arcadia. When we left the English Channel and entered the open sea, the weather was beautiful for the first few days. The sun was shining all day, the sea was calm, and it was a pleasure to travel. Above our heads flew loudly-shrieking flocks of seagulls, and in the water whole herds of dolphins accompanied our ship as if they had

never seen a boat before. When about half-way across the Atlantic, the weather suddenly changed one evening and a storm broke out, a real hurricane accompanied by a deluge of rain. In no time the sea was transformed into high mountains with white tops. One moment we were on top of these foaming mountains and the next we were thrown into what seemed a bottomless abyss...The ballast shifted, and our boat began to list to one side...People were holding on tightly to their iron bedsteads, and many started to pray, and until all became seasick. The seamen apparently anticipated the storm, because they herded us all below deck and closed the hatches. Passengers who had been warned about seasickness before they started the voyage were also told that garlic, onions, whiskey, and Hoffmann's drops were good remedies against seasickness. People were not overly stingy with these remedies, and they partook of them as much as they could stand. As a result of them, such terrible smells developed deck during the storm that even the stewards who ventured in became sick. They swore and cursed, but as they did it in German, which few people understood, it had little effect.

The storm lasted three days without a break, and somehow we survived it without great losses. Only two persons died, an old man and a child. On the fourth day the storm stopped as suddenly as it had started. People breathed in relief and all went to sleep exhausted. Suddenly, during the night, a loud blast and a shock which rattled our iron bedsteads woke us up. People were asking, frightened, "What happened?" Those who could, hurried to the top deck, and were amazed to learn that the boat was surrounded by ice. The crew was patching up a hole below, pumps were throbbing, and our boat was trying to free itself from the icy embrace by moving backwards and forwards. The siren was blowing all the time to prevent eventual collision with some other boat, because it was foggy and one could hardly see a few yards ahead.

We remained ice-bound until morning. The boat was imprisoned by the ice and could not move. The captain ordered all passengers on deck, and we obeyed the order. Bodrug interpreted the captain's commands. We were ordered, when the whistle blew, to run from one side of the boat to the other as fast as we could, and back again. We repeated this maneuver many times. The boat began to sway, broke the ice which was surrounding it, and began to move forward slowly. Our baggage, which was stored below, became soaking wet during that storm, and we suffered great losses.

We wrestled with the ice floes for three days, and only on the fourth day we reached the open sea, which was as clam and smooth as a mirror. After another two and half days of sailing against the wind on the St. Lawrence, we finally reached Quebec and Canada. We had been at sea twenty-one days... [pp. 192-3 of Kaye - they arrived May 2, 1897]

The party of 633 were loaded into ten railway cars and headed to their new homes in the Canadian west.[70]

- Dmytro Romanchych

The Passenger List

Over the course of the 19th century the passenger list evolved and by 1860, the name, age, sex, occupation and national origin of all passengers was collected and recorded. There were two passenger lists for Veronica's voyage; the departure passenger list from Hamburg, Germany and the arrival passenger list from Montreal, Quebec.

Hamburg Port circa 1900. This is where Veronica departed for Canada.[71]

On the departure passenger list, Veronica states Narodowe, Osterreich as her residence. Some immigrants, like Veronica, may never have been out of their village in their lifetime so when asked, "Where do you live?" they might well have simply answered "Narodowe" not realizing that an official would not know where this was.

We discovered that Narodowe, Osterreich is actually Muzylowice, Galicia in the Austro-Hungarian Empire, or by the German name of Münchenthal, Galizien. Note, the German word for Austria is "Osterreich".

Muzylowice has two sides to the village; Muzylowice Narodowe and Muzylowice Kolonia. The full village name would be "Muzylowice Narodowe, Galicia, Austria" and the other side is "Muzylowice Kolonia, Galizien, Osterreich". The inhabitants today still refer to one side of the village as the Colony and the other side as the Village despite no colonists having lived there for more than 70 years.

Galizien (Galicia) was a crown land (province) of the Austrian Empire and after 1867 it was the Austro-Hungarian Empire. Today, the village is the Ukrainian name, "Muzhylovychi".

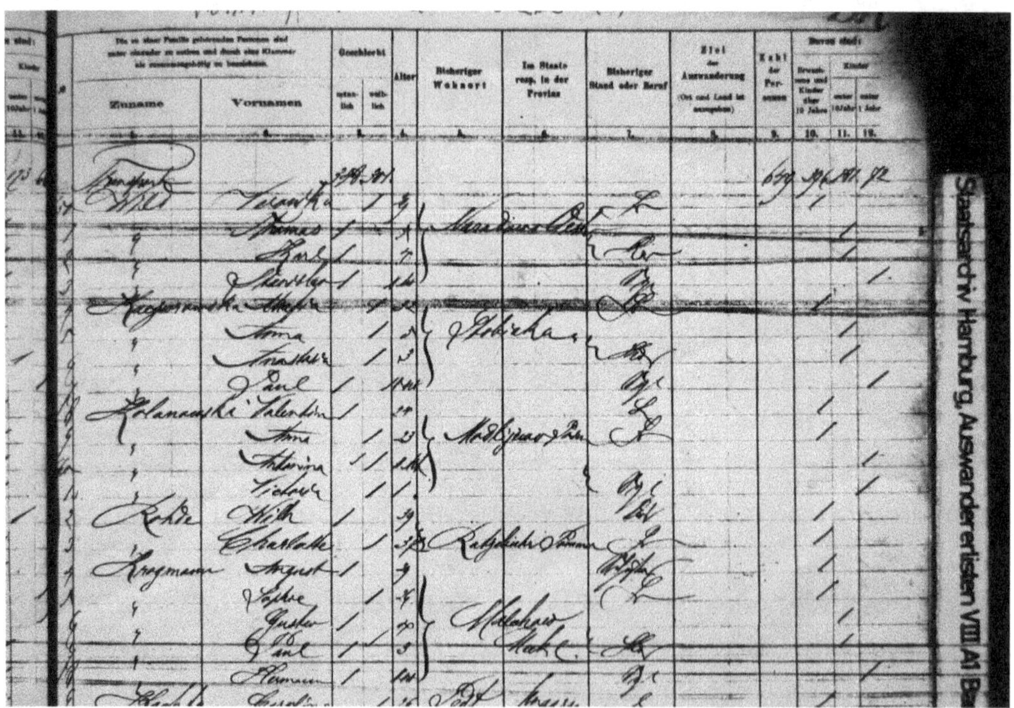

Hamburg Departure Passenger List (copy of original) showing Veronica's residence as "Narodowe Osterreich" (Austria)[72]

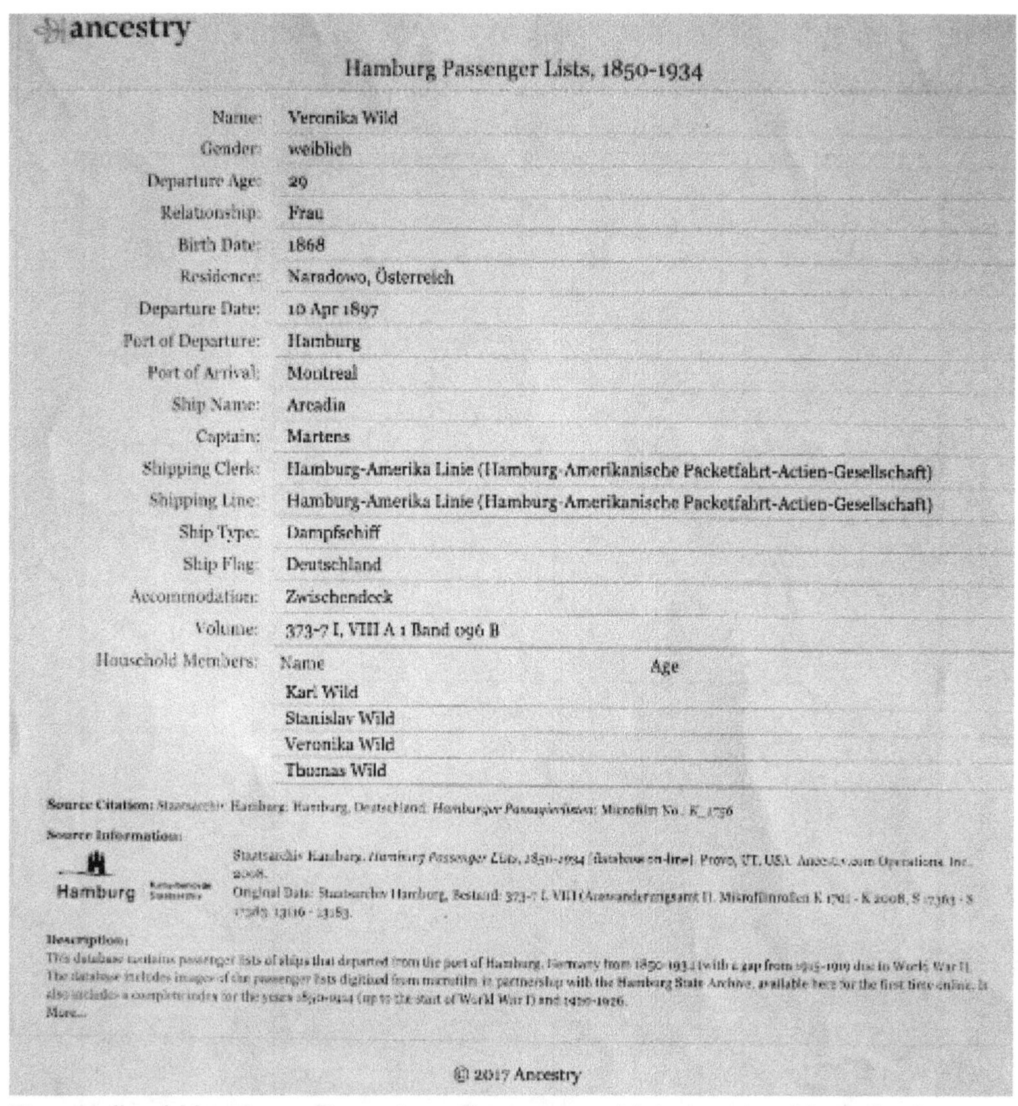

Transcribed Hamburg Departure Passenger List showing Veronica's residence as "Naradowo Osterreich" (Austria) which correctly transcribed is "Narodowe Osterreich".[73]

Veronica may have been aware of the potential for disease when she embarked on her voyage. Her brother and sister in Saskatchewan Canada, may have forewarned her of the more than 20,000 people who died of typhus or "ship fever" from 1847 to 1848, primarily immigrants traveling on steamships. Also, dysentery, smallpox, and scurvy ravaged the transatlantic passengers. [74]

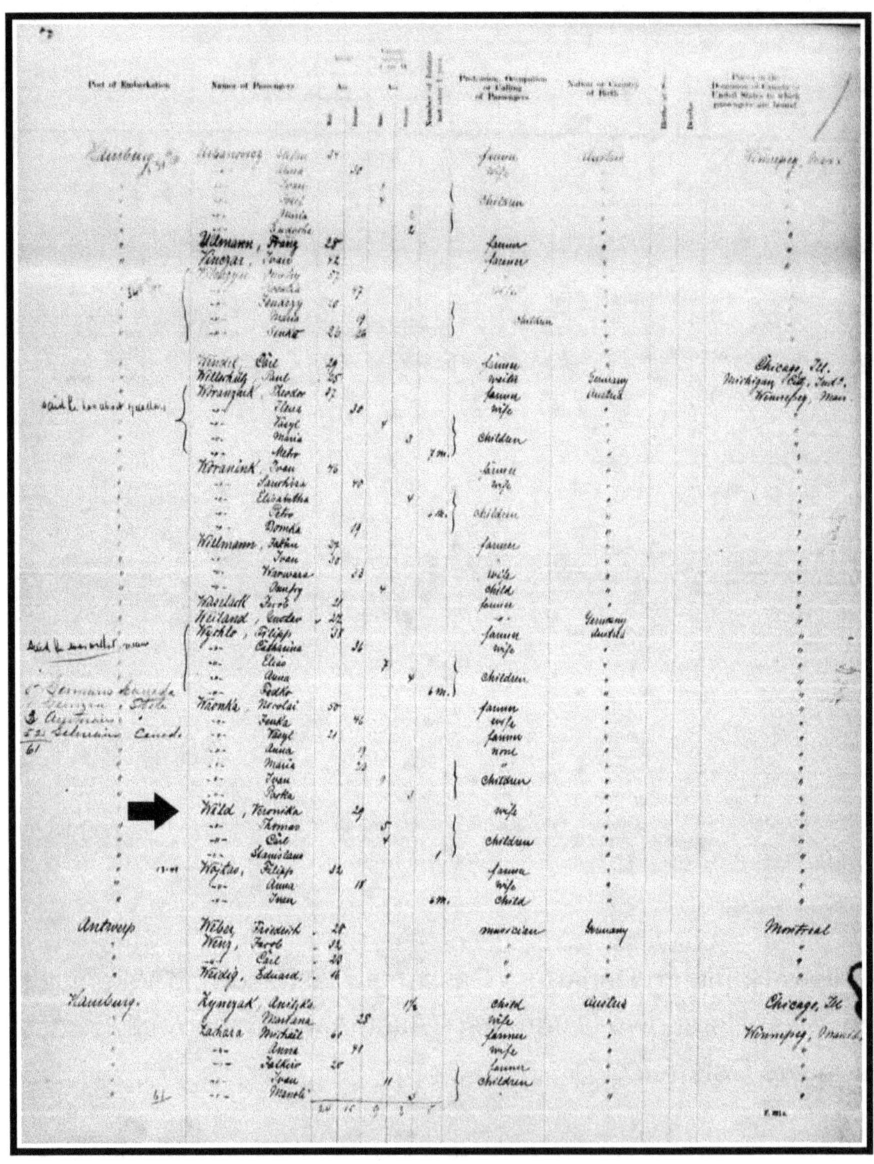

Canada Arrival Passenger List on May 2 1897, Port of Arrival, Montreal Quebec, showing the Veronica Wild family (next to arrow).[75]

Veronica's Little White Lie

On the Hamburg passenger list, it shows the ages of Veronica Wild's three boys as *five years* for Thomas, *four years* for Carl and *eleven months* for Stanislaus. Yet we know for certain each of the boys birth dates, and know the boats sailing date in April, 1897. Therefore, their ages at the time of sailing were actually *nine years* for Thomas, *eight years* for Carl and *three years* for Stanislaus. So why would Veronica tell the official their wrong age?

It may have been financially motivated. As mentioned, the price of a steamer trip was 700 Kronos or approximately $550 in today's currency. Children over five years of age were paying customers. Children under five years of age may have traveled free, so Veronica placed their ages all under five years to get them free ship fare. The families fare was paid by her brother, John Kleczko, living in Canada.

The Kleczko Name and its Variations

Veronica's maiden name, Kleczko, has several variations in the records in Europe. For example, in the 1853 land records, it was spelled Klitszko but the official who wrote the entry had "ch" written over the "z". So Klitszko would be a misspelled Polish version and "Kleschko" would be a German transliteration (putting the sound in German phonetics).

But the true Polish spelling, as Veronica is most likely of Polish descent, and the one used most often in the records is Kleczko. Also, Kleczka might be seen as a female ending with "a". As an example, Kowalski is masculine but Kowalska is feminine in Polish. For English language readers the masculine endings are less confusing, therefore Veronica Kleczko.[76]

Who Emigrated

The region where the Wild's lived is the current Ukraine city of Muzhylovychi. Although the Wild family was stoic German, many of their neighbors were Polish or Ukrainian. There are more Ukrainians in Canada than anywhere outside of Ukraine. Many places, especially in Saskatchewan, were named by ethnic Germans from Ukraine.

The Austrian regions of Galicia and Bukovyna were home to many Germans and Ukrainians. Austrian Galicia was one of the poorest and most overpopulated regions in Europe and had experienced a series of blights and famines. Approximately 170,000 Ukrainian/Germans from the Austro-Hungarian Empire arrived in Canada from September 1891 to August 1914.[77]

The semi-feudal nature of land ownership in the Austro-Hungarian Empire meant that in the "Old Country" people had to pay the *pan* (landlord) for all their firewood and lumber for building. Upon arriving in Canada, the settlers often demanded wooded land from officials so that they would be able to supply their own needs, even if this meant taking land that was less productive for crops. They also attached deep importance to settling near to family, people from nearby villages or other culturally similar groups, furthering the growth of the block settlements.[78]

Arrival to Canada

Immigrants heading to Yorkton, a day's journey away, 1889.[79]

Veronica Kleczko Wild joined her brother, John Kleczko who had taken up farming near Lemberg, Saskatchewan. He had a family of his own to support and life was extremely difficult. Veronica was obliged to work as a domestic to make ends meet and to provide for the children.

The boys were working as hard as grown up men on farms by the time they were ten to twelve years old. They settled near Neudorf, North West Territories (now Saskatchewan, which became a province in 1905) where they were raised.

(l-r) Carl Wild, Thomas Wild, Stanley Wild.[80]

The Wild boys adapted to living in Saskatchewan, losing their German accents and adopting the English language.

Veronica Marries a Second Time

About 1898, Veronica Kleczko Wild married Frank Golling (1873-1943)
who was farming near Lemberg, Saskatchewan. The were married in
Grayson, Saskatchewan. They had four children:

Katherine	1899 - 1974
Mary Florence	1901 - 1974
Elizabeth Ethel	1904 - 1987
Joseph Martin	1908 - 1986

Frank Golling Jr. Family ca. 1904. Veronica Wild Golling is far right.[81]

Back row (l-r): Carl Wild, Stanislaus Wild, Thomas Wild
Front row (l-r): Frank Golling, Mary Golling, Katherine Golling, Veronica
Wild Golling, Elizabeth Golling. (Not yet born: Joseph Martin Golling)

Destination: Lemberg, Saskatchewan

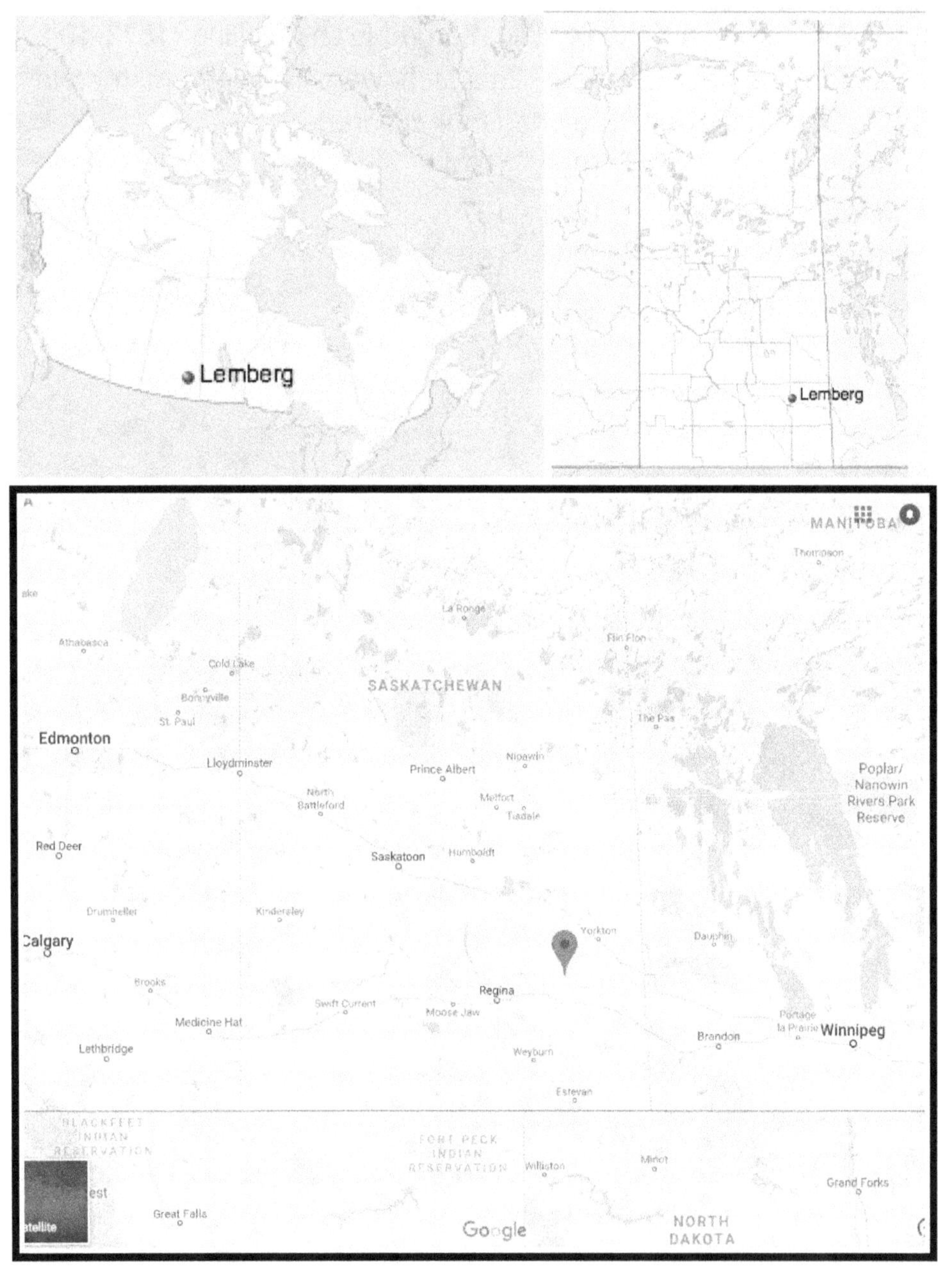

Lemberg, Saskatchewan is east of Regina. It was founded by immigrants from present day L'viv (Ukraine), for which the German name was Lemberg.[82]

Main Street Lemberg, Saskatchewan (SK) in 1906, shown with grain elevator, a landmark for towns of the Prairies.[83]

The town of Lemberg was named after Lemberg in Austria, as most settlers were from that area. Later, the town of Lemberg purchased Frank Golling's land.

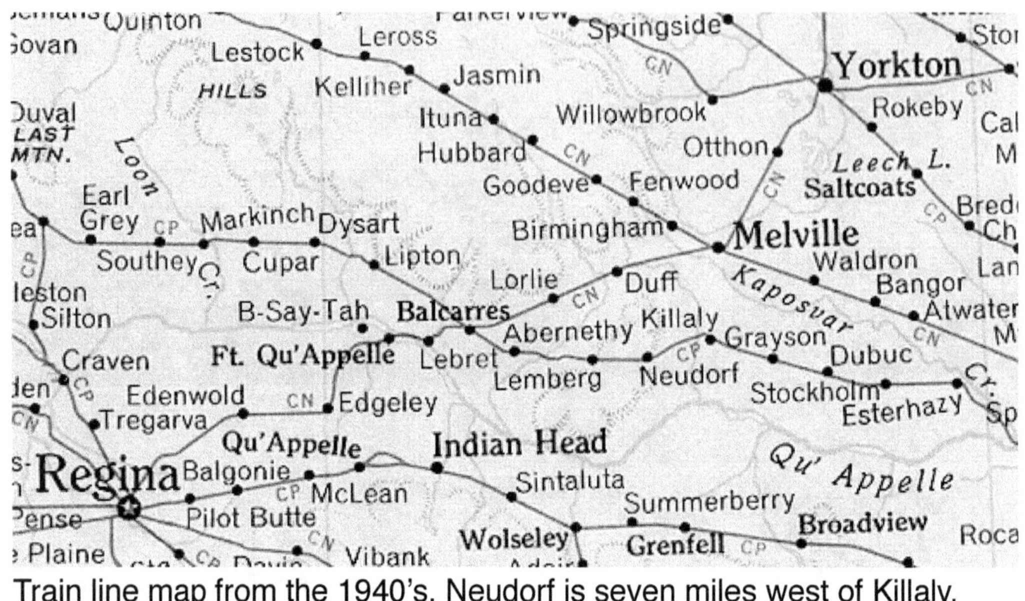

Train line map from the 1940's. Neudorf is seven miles west of Killaly. Lemberg is 17 miles west of Killaly. Grayson is eight miles east.[84]

The next largest community is the town of Melville, the author's birthplace. It is located about 12 miles to the north of Killaly and has a population of 4,500 people. For comparison, Killaly, considered a village, has a population of 74 people.

The grown sons of Franz and Veronica Wild: (l-r) Stanislaus (Stanley) Aloysius Wild, Carl Wild, Thomas John Wild considered Killaly home. [85]

Portrait of the Golling Family with the children grown. Bottom row (l-r): Veronica Golling and Frank Golling .Top row (l-r): Joseph Martin Golling, Elizabeth Ann "Bessie" Golling, Katherine "Kate" Golling, Mary Florence Golling.[86]

Veronicas Birth Date Controversy - The Letter

A letter from Killaly, Saskatchewan to the Muzylowice Roman Catholic Parish in Muzylowice, Austria is in the parish register book with Veronica's birth record. The letter appears to have been written to request a copy of the birth certificate for Veronica Kleczko, born July 2, 1869. Veronica was most likely asking for the birth certificate for purposes of applying for a pension in Canada. It is a rare occurrence to find a letter in Europe requesting a certificate sent from Canada.[87]

The letter from Rev. J. Fuchs, O.M.I. (Missionary Oblates of Mary Immaculate) in Killaly, SK dated July 2, 1937. The upper part of the letter is in Latin as was the case for most Catholic correspondence during that time in history. The lower part of the letter is in German, since the Canadian priest knew Muzylowice was a German colony.[88]

Below is the unique letter translated.[89]

Translation from Latin:
Reverend Parish Priest,
Many greetings in the Lord,

Please send me the document regarding the birth and baptism of this person:

Veronica Kleczko, born on July 2nd, A.D. 1869.

Her parents were Joannes Kleczko and Maria, née Schnerch. But note that Veronica cannot confirm with certainty that she was born in 1869. Therefore, I am not certain whether she was not born one or more years before of after the year 1869.

Please find enclosed in this letter one dollar, as payment for your expenses and efforts.

With fraternal greetings,
Rev. J. Fuchs, O.M.I.

Translation from German:
Highly Honored Confrere,

I don't know whether or not you speak German, therefore I presented above my request in Latin asking for the certificate of baptism, as described above. In case if you do understand German, kindly help out in clarifying this matter. One Canadian dollar is attached here to cover your expenses and the effort to achieve this.

With my greetings in Christ,
Rev. J. Fuchs, O.M.I.

1865				NOMEN	Religio		Sexus		Legitimi / Illegitimi Thori	PARENTES		PATRINI	
Nr. posit.	Mensis		Numerus Domus		Catholica	Aut alia	Puer	Puella		NOMEN	Conditio	NOMEN	Conditio
	Natus	Baptisatus											
15	26	29	118	Josephus	1	.	1	.	Legitimi	Joañes Flöhn — Rosalia fil. Josephi Kisler et Catharina Schmid	Coloni. sta.	Josephus Fmerich — Magdalena uxor — Joañis Brauenberger	Coloni. sta.
16	2	2	154	Veronica	1	.	.	1	Legitimi	Joañes Kletschn — Maria fil. Josephi Knetsch et Joan. bina Josfstadt	Coloni. sta.	Candidus Jesstadt — Ana Zauckish virgo.	Coloni. sta.

This document is part of a page from the Roman Catholic birth register. This registers the birth of Veronica Kleczko, July 2, 1868. The birth registers were books with the title *Liber Natorum*.[90]

The year 1868 is the true year of Veronica's birth because it is on the original entry of birth in the register book. The date is shown in the upper left corner. In Canada, Veronica's birth year of 1869 is incorrect.

> The discrepancy in years is understandable. People remember their age and then they subtract the age from the current year. Often it turns out to be a year either off depending on whether they had already had their birthday that year when they did the calculation. In genealogy, we go with the document/record that is created closest in time to the actual event. So in this case the birth register entry was created in 1868, but the source in Canada would have been created later (or calculated based on age). Of course when something is obviously wrong with an

original entry, then exceptions have to be made, but usually it means finding more than one source that agree with the proposed correct information. But in this case it is clear that her birth was in 1868.[91]

- Brian J. Lenius

The Golling Nurses

Mary Golling upon graduation from nursing school.[92]

Kate Golling upon graduation from nursing school.[93]

Their son, Joe Golling and his family, lived with them during the last years on the farm. After Frank Golling's death in 1943, Veronica went to live with her daughter, Katherine Kleczko Bruch, for some years.

Veronica Wild Golling (1868-1952)[94]

Veronica's last years were spent at a retirement home at St. Hubert's Mission near Whitewood, Saskatchewan. She was very lonesome there and died on October 18, 1952. Veronica is buried at St. Elizabeth Catholic Church Cemetery in Killaly, Saskatchewan.

Veronica Wild Golling's tombstone at St. Elizabeth's Roman Catholic Church cemetery, Killaly, Saskatchewan.[95]

This wonderful woman, who is the matriarch of the Wilde family in Canada and the United States, now rests in peace in Killaly, Saskatchewan, where she called home.

Chapter 2. Scotland to Nova Scotia

Scottish Roots

Many of our MacDonald ancestors emigrated from the Isle of Eigg, Inner Hebrides Islands in the Highlands of Scotland.

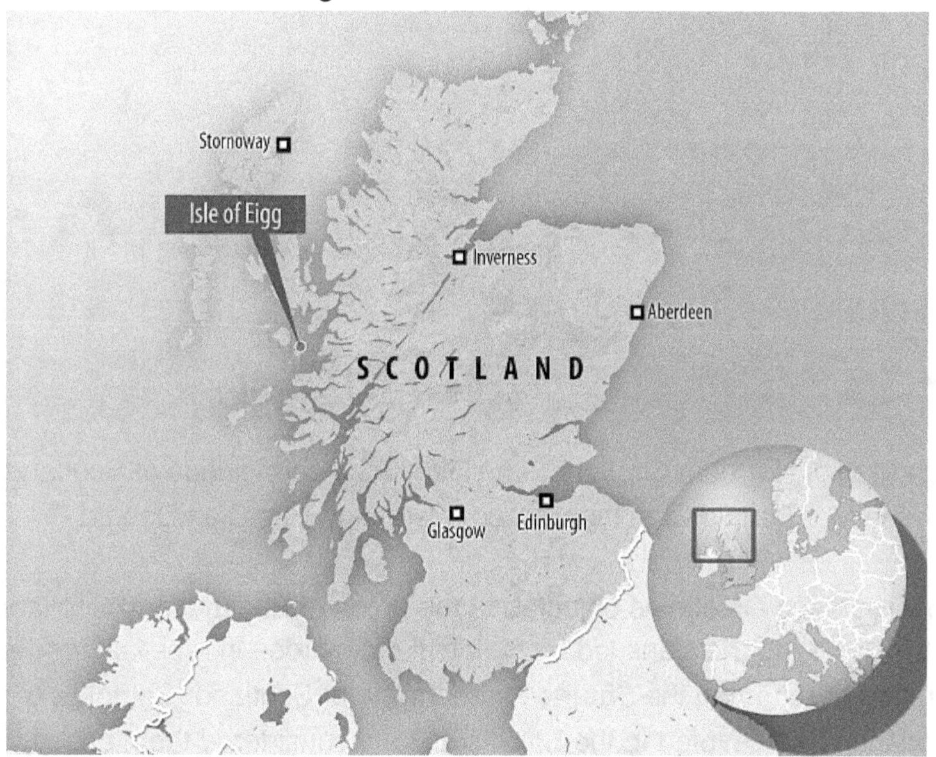

Location of Isle of Eigg, Hebridean Islands, Scotland.[96]

On the mainland directly east of Isle of Eigg is the town of Arisaig, Scotland. It's counterpart in Canada is Arisaig, Nova Scotia named after the Scottish town. Many of the MacDonald clan from Isle of Eigg settled in Prince Edward Island and Nova Scotia, Canada.

Clan Map of Northern Scotland; The Highlands and Islands of Scotland, with the MacDonald Clan highlighted. Also known as Clan Donald.[97]

Most Highland Chieftains objected to the union of England and Scotland. In 1715 to 1745 the clans led by their Chieftains rose in rebellion for the purpose of returning the Stuarts to the throne of Scotland. Catholics of Scotland were devoted to the Stuarts as they considered them priestly entitled to the throne of Great Britain. Loyalty to the rightful sovereigns was a duty entrusted by the Church. However, English soldiers took possession of the Highlands and attempted to keep the clans down.

One of the officers of the British Army was Major James Wolf who later became the hero of Louisbourg and Quebec. He had observed the bravery of the Highlanders and was instrumental in having many Highlanders enlist in the British army. Thus the Highlander regiment was sent to America where they noted the richness of the land as compared to Scotland. Some of the Highlanders were banished to the USA after the Battle of Culloden (1746) in which Prince Charles was defeated.[98]

They were active in the Battle of the Plains of Abraham (1759), part of the Seven Years War which resulted in the cession of Canada to Britain. These men settled in St. John's Island now known as Prince Edward Island.

Crest of Clan MacDonald. Clan Motto: *Per mare per terras* which means "by sea and by land".[99]

About 1763 many Highland hands were disbanded as a new economic system was embraced. The clans were no longer required for military purposes as many baronies were turned into sheep farms and many families were driven across the stormy Atlantic in rotten boats to seek a new home in the forests of America.

About 1770, Captain John MacDonald of Glenaladale came to the assistance of his Catholic fellowman in Scotland who were being pursued by their landlords to abandon their faith. He assisted the poor people to return to Glasgow and other towns; finally charting a vessel in Edinburgh to take them to Prince Edward Island.

In 1773, more Scottish immigrants came to Pictou and Prince Edward Island from South Uist, the second largest island of the Outer Hebrides in Scotland, and Glengarry, on the mainland of Scotland.

Coat of Arms Clan MacDonald and high chief Clan Donald.[100]

Isle of Eigg today. [101]

In 1776 the American war stopped emigration until 1790 at which time the exodus from Scotland was so great that leading men in Scotland attempted to stay. It was feared that very few people would be left on the great estates of Clanranald or Glengarry.

DNA Tests and Scottish Ethnicity

As part of our family history research and discovery, DNA tests were conducted to estimate our historical ethnicity.[102] These results show the mapped genetic communities in Scotland and Nova Scotia. For more information see *DNA Test Results* in Appendix X.

Early History of Nova Scotia

The province of Nova Scotia, which means "New Scotland" in Scottish Gaelic, was settled in the following order: The Micmacs, the French and the English.

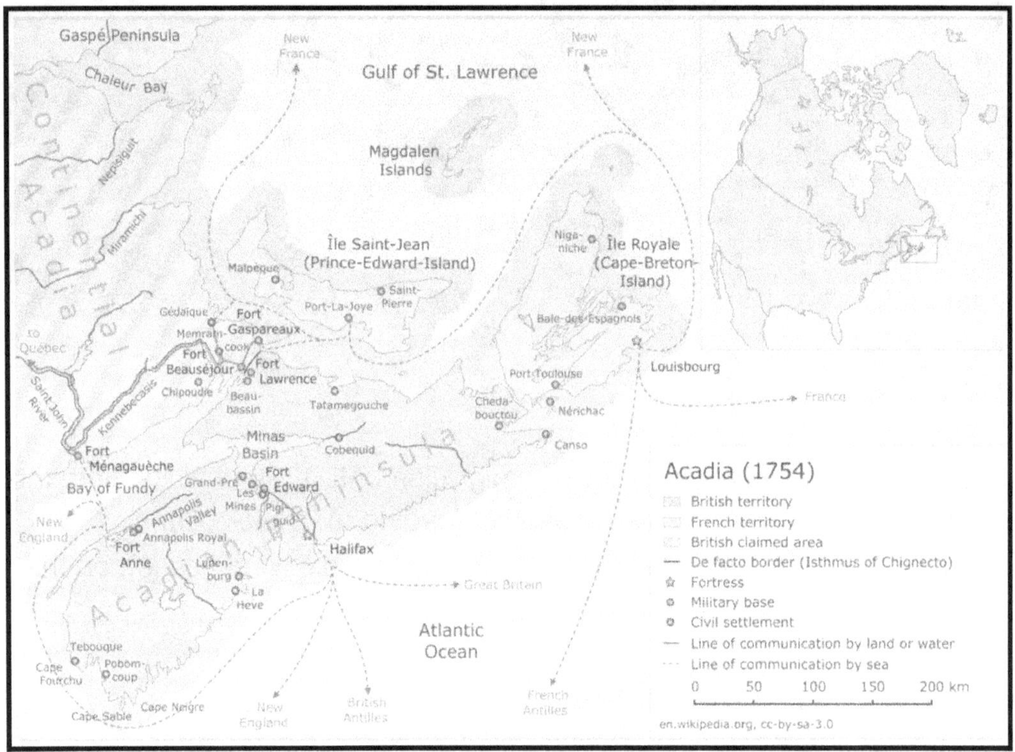

Historical Map Acadia 1754.[103]

Several historical highlights are:

- Treaty of Utrecht (1713) in which Louis XV ceded Acadia to England but reserved "L'Isle Royale" or Cape Breton on which he built a stronghold named Louisbourg, completed in 1720.

- Recollects from France arrived at Louisbourg about 1718 where they served the military as chaplains and were pastors to the inhabitants.

- The Seminary of Foreign Missions of France establishes the branch of Seminary of Quebec.

- In 1758 the English destroyed Louisbourg and its churches including Marguerite Bourgeoys convent, and its hospital. Priests and religious communities were banished, leaving utter desolation. Inhabitants fled to St. Pierre and Miquelon islands for their safety.

- In 1759 the colonies made peace with the English.

Painting of Louisbourg, the fortified town on Île Royale (Cape Breton Island).[104] The fall of Louisbourg to the British in 1758 paved the way for the capture of Québec and the end of French rule in North America.

Prince Edward Island, Nova Scotia and Cape Breton Island were predominantly Gaelic-speaking. It is estimated more than 50,000 Gaelic settlers from Scotland immigrated to Nova Scotia and Cape Breton Island between 1815 and 1870.

Until 1817 the jurisdiction over Nova Scotia and Cape Breton Island was transferred from the Bishop of Isuches to the Right Reverend Edmund Burke, Bishop of Petria. There were only five missions of which Arisaig, Nova Scotia was one.

The census of 1871 indicated 140,694 people lived on Nova Scotia and Cape Breton Island, of which 93,901 were Scots, 15,000 French, 14,794 Irish, 11,837 English and others.

The French controlled islands of Saint Pierre and Miquelon near Newfoundland and Labrador had a history of Acadian migration. Many French emigrated from Miquelon to Nova Scotia. Saint Pierre and Miquelon remain a French territory to this day.

New Settlers in Arisaig

Arisaig was the first settlement made in the county of Antigonish by Scotch emigrants. The first white man to come to Arisaig was Angus McDonald from Morar, Scotland. His real surname was Gillis, but he changed it to McDonald. He took up to 500 acres of land at Arisaig but due to the hostility of the Indians, moved to Merigomish, Nova Scotia where his descendants live to this day.

His brother, John Ban Gillis became the first permanent settler in Arisaig.

Donald McDonald (Red), our ancestor, came out in 1791 and settled on a farm west of the farm of John Ban Gillis on the gulf.

The first Catholic Chapel in Antigonish was built in 1810. At this time, Bishop Plessis named the new mission St. Ninian's in 1812. Later, Saint Ninian's Roman Catholic Cathedral was built between 1867 to 1886 in

Antigonish, Nova Scotia, an imposing Romanesque Revival architectural design.

Arisaig, Nova Scotia, a coastal town where our MacDonald family lived.[105] Antigonish, a college town today, is 18 miles inland from Arisaig.

The Church in Arisaig

St. Margaret's Roman Catholic Church in Arisaig was the earliest Highland Catholic mission in Nova Scotia and was the home parish to our ancestors.

In the year 1792 the first primitive church was built on the site that is now beach near the present Arisaig Pier. It was made of logs and was constructed in one day. Reverend James McDonald was the first resident pastor, but due to poor health went to Quebec, where after a few years he died.

St. Margaret's Church, Arisaig, Nova Scotia. It's the oldest Roman Catholic parish in Nova Scotia named after St. Margaret of Scotland.[106]

For seven years after Fr. James MacDonald's retirement, the people of Arisaig looked to the clergy of Prince Edward Island for spiritual guidance. Fr. Angus McEachern from PEI used to visit Arisaig once a year where he spent a couple of weeks with marriages, baptisms and the administration of the sacraments. He then visited the other missions in the county. As no one died in those days without the rites of the church, he was frequently brought across the strait in a boat on sick calls.

In 1802, Father Alexander MacDonald came from Scotland and settled in Arisaig as resident pastor of the missions. Bishop Plessis visited Arisaig in 1812 and found Fr. Alexander in charge of 350 Highland families in addition to several missions. The Bishop found him comfortably settled in

Arisaig and expressed astonishment at finding so much comfort and elegance in such a new and isolated place. However, Fr. Alexander was the chief man of the place and he, therefore had to entertain the notabilities of the country. His Highland parishioners were proud of him as their pastor and leader and furnished him with every comfort. As a representative of character he paid annual visits to Halifax and held consultations with the Governor and other ruling powers. He was able to secure political favors for his people, one of these being the first wharf or pier of Arisaig. This pier afforded shelter to boats and small vessels from violent gales during autumn. A more modern pier has since replaced the original.

Bishop Plessis was very impressed with the Highlanders. On the day of his departure, crowds followed him to the pier to received a last benediction from him. He had only spent a few days with them and he could not speak a word of their language and they could not understand a word of his; nevertheless their faith was predominant.

Trunk Road Arisaig to Antigonish, Nova Scotia 1873.[107]

The Right Reverend Edmund Burke in 1818 as Bishop of Sion was the next to visit Arisaig. He was well remembered for his charity to the poor, the prisoners and the Micmacs (Indian Tribe) at the time of his death in Halifax.

Dr. Burke was a native of County Kildare, Ireland. He was a professor of Philosophy and Mathematics in Quebec for several years. He studied in Paris and rose to eminent distinction in the University of Paris for his knowledge in mathematical science and proficiency in Latin, Greek and Hebrew. While in Quebec, Lord Worchester requested his assistance in pacifying the Indian tribes about Lake Superior and parts of Ohio and Louisiana who were hostile to the British government. For seven years he worked among the Indians converting them to Christianity and to the loyal citizens. In return the British government gave him a pension for life and it is said British Ministers were influential with the See of Rome in obtaining his title of Bishop.

In 1816 Fr. Alexander MacDonald died and was succeeded by his assistant until 1818.

Money was scarce in this region. For church dues, the parishioners paid with potatoes traded for cash in Newfoundland.

The Highlanders were a strong, hardy race, strong in faith with unspoiled and simple dispositions. Their hearts were exalted in the sense of freedom and emancipation from petty prosecution. On Sunday they flocked to church from far and wide where they had a confab in Gaelic.

Stage coach passing through Antigonish, Nova Scotia.[108]

In the year 1828, Neil McLeod returned to Antigonish. Bishop Fraser succeeded in obtaining the privilege of sending students to the Scots College in Rome. These young men, including Neil, left for Rome and after a difficult voyage finally arrived. Rome was the home of peace, science and religion. Leo XII was the reigning Pope at the time.

In 1837, Neil McLeod was ordained and returned to take charge of East Bay, Nova Scotia on Cape Breton Island where he stayed all his life. He solicited government aid in building a bridge across the head of the bay and in the construction of a church.

St. Margaret's Church 1903. Inset Fr. Ronald MacDougall parish priest[109]

Early School in Arisaig

The first school was situated at Ardnafuaran, two miles from Arisaig. The schoolhouse was made of logs, with fireplaces extended from side to side, the roof covered with tar paper. The teacher was Stephen MacDonald, father of Donald MacDonald. The students used birch bark for writing paper, quill was used for pens, and the book *"Thomas Dilworth's Spelling Book"* was learned.[110]

The teacher usually lived upstairs and the students brought milk to him as a goodwill gesture. Sometimes an additional room in the schoolhouse was used for selling rum.

Latin, Greek and Algebra requirements were essential for teaching. Malcolm McLellan, a graduate of high school in Glasgow, Scotland taught Latin and Greek to students.

Government aid was sought by Rev W.B. McLead. There was difficulty in obtaining books, especially Latin ones.

St. Francis Xavier College originated with a gift of 500 acres valued at $3,000 by Angus and Samuel MacDonald (St. Andrews).

The Casket, a weekly newspaper publication was started in 1852 by John Boyd of Antigonish who set up a printing press and also started a Catholic book store. The "Casket" name referred to a woman's jewelry box.

Train station Antigonish, Nova Scotia.[111] Nova Scotia means "New Scotland" in Latin.

The MacDonald Family Heritage:

Donald (Tailor) MacDonald (Mary Ann MacDonald Wilde's great grandfather) was also known as Tailor Pioneer because of having worked in this capacity of a tailor for the army in Scotland. He came to Canada from the Isle of Eigg about the year 1800.

Donald was married twice; first to Isabella MacDonald; and secondly, to Annie MacDonald.

An Sgurr and Galmisdale farm, Isle of Eigg Scotland c.1880[112]

George MacDonald (Mary Ann MacDonald Wilde's grandfather) was the son of Donald MacDonald. He too married twice, first to Annie MacDonald and after her death to Mary MacDonald.

Ann MacDonald (Mary Ann Wilde's mother) and was the daughter of George MacDonald with his second wife, Mary MacDonald.

Donald (Red) MacDonald, son of Angus MacDonald was born in Glengarry County, Ontario in 1787 and went to Arisaig, Nova Scotia in 1791. He married Catherine MacInnis, daughter of Angus MacInnis. They had two children, Alexander and Elizabeth.

Alexander MacDonald married Catherine MacDonald who had eight children, one of which was John A. MacDonald.

Lineage Charts of the MacDonald Family

The lineage charts outline Mary Ann MacDonald's family, including siblings, parents, grandparents and great-grandparents.[113] The lineage chart of Thomas and Mary Ann Wilde includes their children.

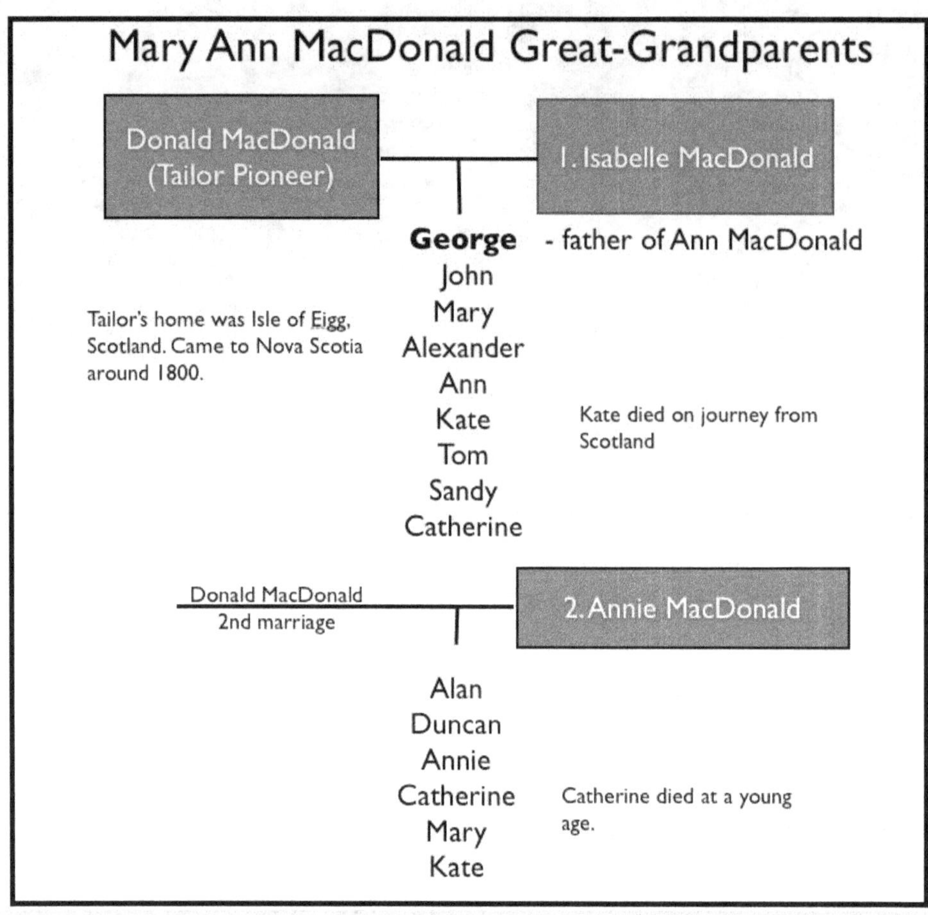

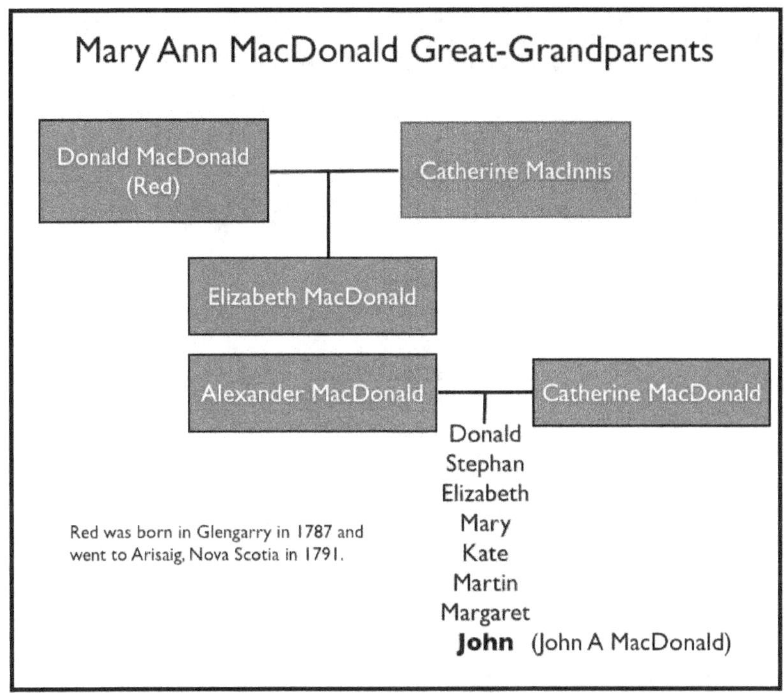

Mary Ann MacDonald Great-Grandparents
Donald MacDonald (Red)
Catherine MacInnis
Elizabeth MacDonald
Alexander MacDonald
Catherine MacDonald
Donald
Stephan
Elizabeth
Mary
Kate
Martin
Margaret
John   (John A MacDonald)
Red was born in Glengarry in 1787 and went to Arisaig, Nova Scotia in 1791.

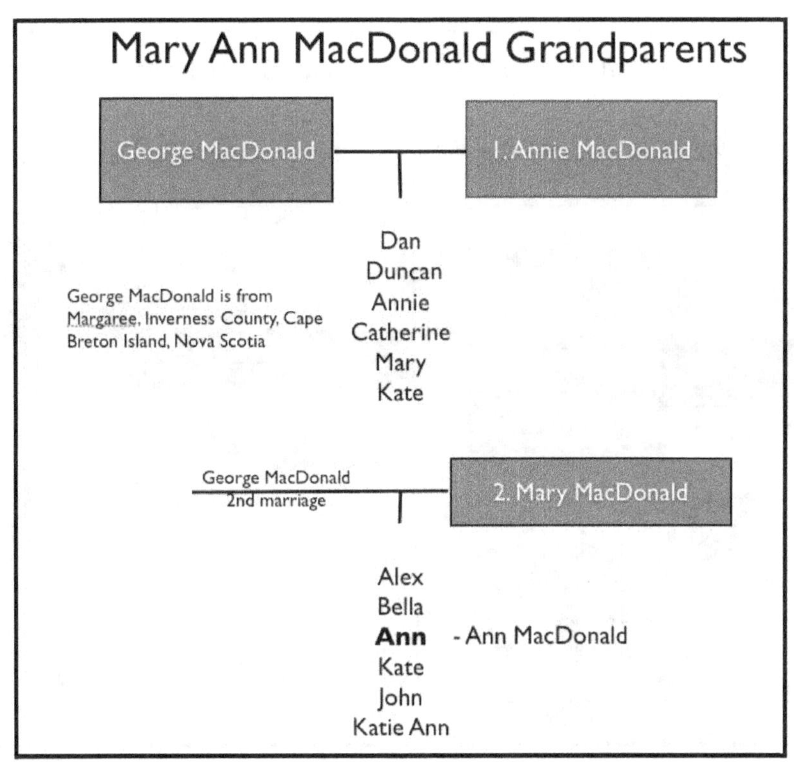

Mary Ann MacDonald Grandparents
George MacDonald
1. Annie MacDonald
Dan
Duncan
Annie
Catherine
Mary
Kate
George MacDonald is from Margaree, Inverness County, Cape Breton Island, Nova Scotia
George MacDonald 2nd marriage
2. Mary MacDonald
Alex
Bella
Ann   - Ann MacDonald
Kate
John
Katie Ann

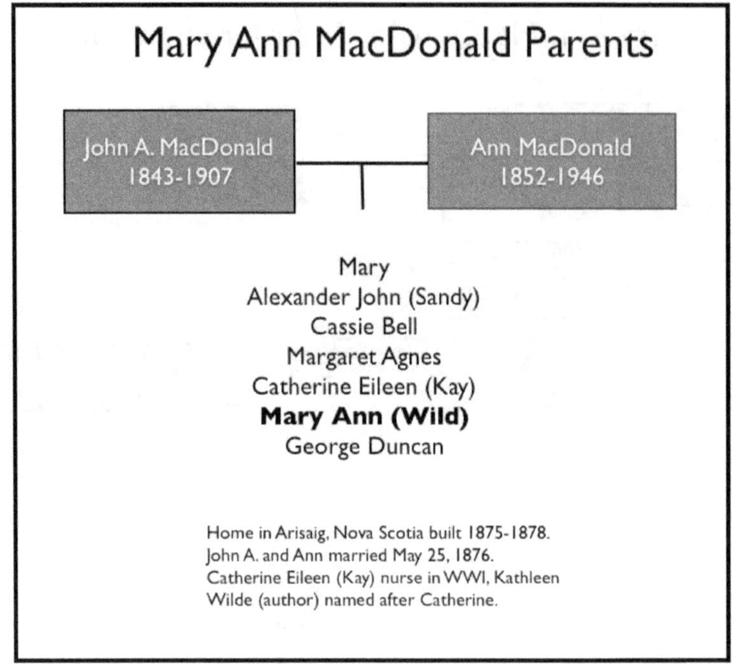

Mary Ann MacDonald Parents

John A. MacDonald
1843-1907

Ann MacDonald
1852-1946

Mary
Alexander John (Sandy)
Cassie Bell
Margaret Agnes
Catherine Eileen (Kay)
Mary Ann (Wild)
George Duncan

Home in Arisaig, Nova Scotia built 1875-1878.
John A. and Ann married May 25, 1876.
Catherine Eileen (Kay) nurse in WWI, Kathleen
Wilde (author) named after Catherine.

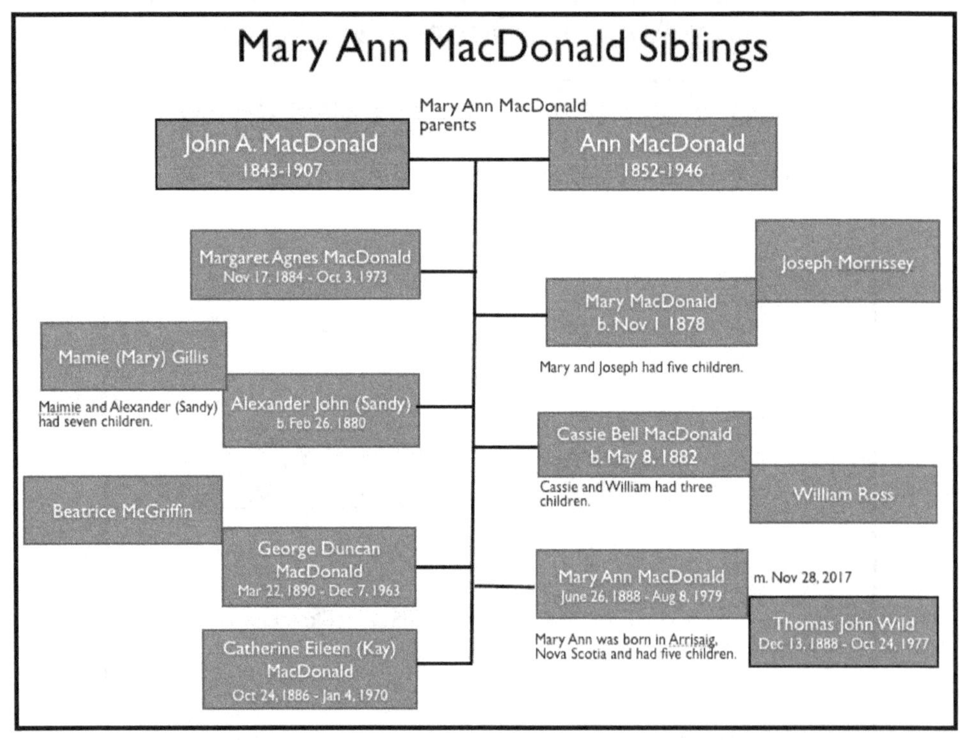

Mary Ann MacDonald Siblings

Mary Ann MacDonald
parents

John A. MacDonald
1843-1907

Ann MacDonald
1852-1946

Margaret Agnes MacDonald
Nov 17, 1884 - Oct 3, 1973

Joseph Morrissey

Mary MacDonald
b. Nov 1 1878

Mamie (Mary) Gillis

Mary and Joseph had five children.

Maimie and Alexander (Sandy)
had seven children.

Alexander John (Sandy)
b. Feb 26, 1880

Cassie Bell MacDonald
b. May 8, 1882

Beatrice McGriffin

Cassie and William had three
children.

William Ross

George Duncan
MacDonald
Mar 22, 1890 - Dec 7, 1963

Mary Ann MacDonald
June 26, 1888 - Aug 8, 1979

m. Nov 28, 2017

Thomas John Wild
Dec 13, 1888 - Oct 24, 1977

Mary Ann was born in Arisaig,
Nova Scotia and had five children.

Catherine Eileen (Kay)
MacDonald
Oct 24, 1886 - Jan 4, 1970

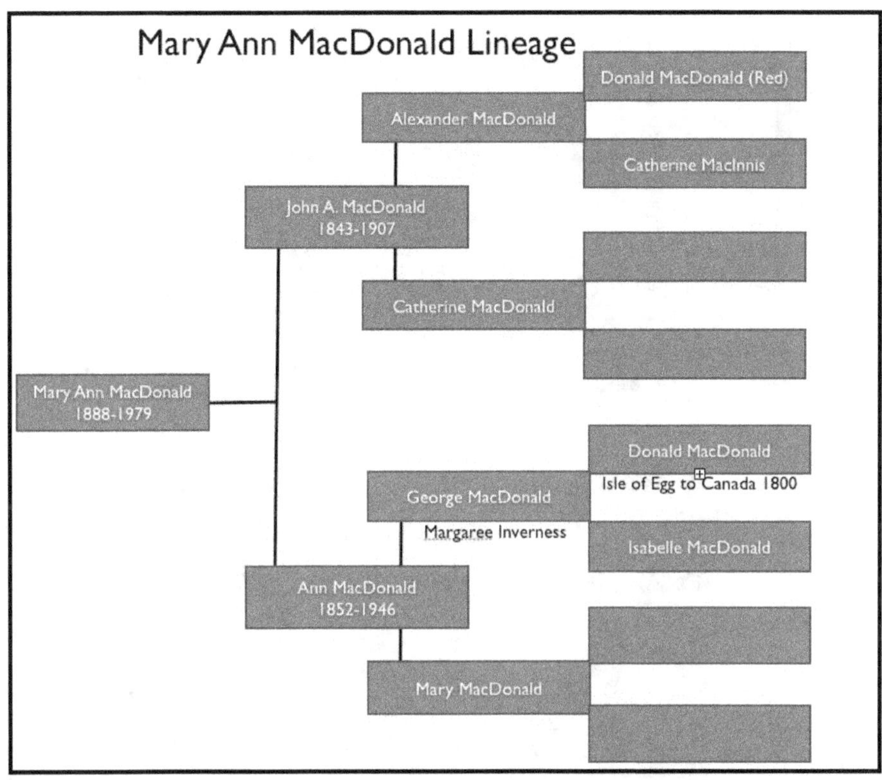

Mary Ann MacDonald Lineage
Donald MacDonald (Red)
Alexander MacDonald
Catherine MacInnis
John A. MacDonald
1843-1907
Catherine MacDonald
Mary Ann MacDonald
1888-1979
Donald MacDonald
Isle of Egg to Canada 1800
George MacDonald
Margaree Inverness
Isabelle MacDonald
Ann MacDonald
1852-1946
Mary MacDonald

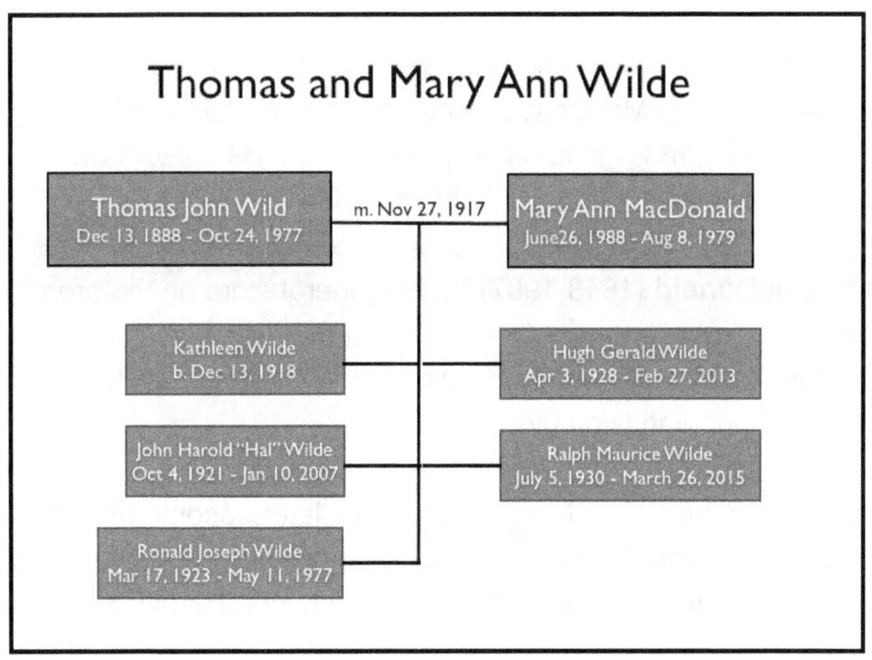

Thomas and Mary Ann Wilde
Thomas John Wild
Dec 13, 1888 - Oct 24, 1977
m. Nov 27, 1917
Mary Ann MacDonald
June26, 1988 - Aug 8, 1979
Kathleen Wilde
b. Dec 13, 1918
Hugh Gerald Wilde
Apr 3, 1928 - Feb 27, 2013
John Harold "Hal" Wilde
Oct 4, 1921 - Jan 10, 2007
Ralph Maurice Wilde
July 5, 1930 - March 26, 2015
Ronald Joseph Wilde
Mar 17, 1923 - May 11, 1977

John A. MacDonald family.[114]
First row: (l-r) Alexander (Sandy), John A. MacDonald, Ann MacDonald
with George Duncan MacDonald, Catherine (Kay) MacDonald, Mary Ann
MacDonald, Margaret Agnes MacDonald, Cassie Bell MacDonald.
Standing: Mary MacDonald, a cousin. ca. 1894.

John A. MacDonald (1843-1907) had a general store on the premise of
his home in Arisaig. John A. MacDonald married Ann MacDonald
(1850-1946) on May 23, 1876 and they would go on to have seven
children; five girls and two boys.

One of the girls, Mary Ann MacDonald would later become Mary Ann Wild
(1888-1979), mother of Kathleen Wilde (author), Ralph Maurice Wilde,
Hugh Gerald Wilde, Ronald Joseph Wilde and John Harold "Hal" Wilde.

By coincidence, John A. had the same exact name as the first Prime Minister of Canada, Sir John A. MacDonald, who is considered the founding father of Canada. Sir John brought together the provinces of Upper and Lower Canada, Nova Scotia and New Brunswick in 1867 to form Canada.

John A. MacDonald home, Arisaig, Nova Scotia where Mary Ann MacDonald was born.[115]

John A. MacDonald was a hard worker and much respected in the community. In those days, John A. was considered one of the more progressive people in the area. Progress was measured not by the model of car owned, but on the horse carriages driven. As horses were the main means of transportation, they were always well groomed and used with fine carriages.

Horse and carriage used for "Sunday" travel. ca. 1912[116]

John A's health condition deteriorated in his later years and he developed ulcers of the stomach. It was suggested that he undergo surgery for this condition, but medical expertise at that time had not advanced to that of today and very few survived major surgery. John A. decided not to go this route and passed away at the age of 64.

George MacDonald (Mary Ann's grandfather) was the son of Donald MacDonald. He too was married twice, first to Annie MacDonald and after her death to Mary MacDonald.

Ann MacDonald (1852-1946) (Mary Ann's mother)
Ann MacDonald was the daughter of George MacDonald and his second wife Mary MacDonald.

A young Ann MacDonald, Mary Ann MacDonald's mother.[117]

As mentioned, Ann married John A. MacDonald in 1876 and they resided in Arisaig, Nova Scotia, living in comfortable circumstances since John was proprietor of the local general store. After John A. died in 1907, Ann had to assume responsibility for the household.

Her son Sandy was a great help to her. Cassie Bell (Ross) and her three children lived in the old home in Arisaig with her for some years.

During World War II, the Ross family moved to New Glasgow and Ann went to live with her daughter, Catherine Eileen in Halifax. They lived in an apartment off Ivenpool Road. Here Ann was to spend her last days passing her time with needlework and watching the people from her window coming and going on the street car.

Ann MacDonald at her favorite pastime, needlework.[118]

Alexander (Sandy) MacDonald (1880-1934) was the eldest son of John Alexander and Ann MacDonald. Sandy lived in Arisaig, Nova Scotia. He was a great help to his mother after his father's death. He was married to Mamie Gillis and they had seven children; six girls and one boy. Their home was on the top of a hill within sight of St. Margaret's Church in Arisaig.

Alexander (Sandy) MacDonald, Mary Ann MacDonald's eldest brother.[119]

When the co-op was being introduced in Nova Scotia, he played an active part in it's organization.

Times were hard in the 1930's. At Easter time, Sandy was getting a cured ham out of a barrel of brine for a neighbour. The brine, in which the ham was cured, caused his hand to become infected. The infection spread to his arm and it was necessary that it be amputated in an attempt to save his life. However, he died in St. Martha's Hospital in Antigonish at the age of 54 in the year 1934.

Sandy's death was a great loss, his family being so young and his mother being advanced in age; all of whom depended on him.

George Duncan MacDonald (1890-1963) was the youngest of the John A. MacDonald family. George was 17 years old when his father died. He thought highly of his father and missed him a lot.

George attended St. Francis Xavier University in Antigonish where he obtained a Bachelor of Arts degree. There were no jobs in Nova Scotia for a young man so qualified so when his two sisters, Mary Ann and Margaret, decided to go west in search of teaching positions, he decided to go with them. There was a demand for teachers in British Columbia for qualified people and the Roman Catholic Church invited graduates from St. Francis Xavier College to fill this vacuum and George was among those who responded to this call.

However, he did not like teaching and sought employment in other fields. These included being a timekeeper in the Coalhurst mine at Lethbridge, Alberta, a job he later recommended to his brother-in-law, Joe Morrissey. He often marveled at how Joe brought up a family of five on that job.

George worked for the John Deer Company and it was during his days traveling throughout Saskatchewan that he witnessed the dire poverty and hardship of the rural people, many of whom were immigrants who had come to Canada in search of new homes. These were the days of the Great Depression (1929-1939) under the conservatives and liberal governments of R.B. Bennett and Mackenzie King. Like many in the west, George saw the inhumane way these governments treated the unemployed and impoverished farmers. Times were hard and living in hotels while traveling throughout the province made for difficult living. He favored the socialist government of the CCJ and was a great admirer of Tommy Douglas, a great conversationalist, who became premier of Saskatchewan.

While filling the position of collection manager for the John Deer Company he married Beatrice McGiffin (Bea). She pre deceased him in 1952.

When George retired he invited his niece, Mary Ross from Nova Scotia to live with him. Mary had been very ill and her mother had died. This proved to be a very happy arrangement for them both.

George was later afflicted with leukemia and it was a great satisfaction to have Mary Rose there.

George Duncan MacDonald died on December 7, 1963 and is buried in the Catholic Cemetery in Saskatoon, Saskatchewan.

Catherine (Kay) Eileen MacDonald (1886-1970) was the fifth child of John A. MacDonald and Ann MacDonald.

Catherine (Kay) Eileen MacDonald upon graduation from nursing school.[120]

Like her sisters, Kay attended Mount St. Bernard in Antigonish, an all girls school founded in 1883 by Bishop Cameron and entrusted into the hands of the Congregation de Notre Dame. She later trained as a Registered Nurse at St. Martha's hospital in Antigonish.

Catherine (Kay) Eileen MacDonald in WWI nurse uniform.[121]

Kathleen (Kay) Wilde, (the author) was named after Catherine (Kay) Eileen MacDonald, her aunt. During WWI (1914-1918) Catherine served as a nursing sister in France. Since Kathleen was born while Kay was overseas, she was named after her aunt in case she did not come back from the war.

After the war, Catherine returned to Halifax and worked in the Camp Hill Hospital until she retired. She was well known and greatly admired by all who were in contact with her, especially military people.

She was very generous to those in need and cared for her mother in her later years.

Upon retirement, she was free to travel throughout Canada, but always returned to Halifax.

Mary Ann MacDonald (1888-1979) was the daughter of John Alexander MacDonald, who was a general merchant in Arisaig, Nova Scotia. The family members assisted in the store operations when old enough. As there were five girls in the family, a dressmaker was hired, usually in the spring, to make the necessary clothes and while doing this she stayed in the home. The MacDonald girls were responsible for looking after their own belongings, hence were not allowed to wear each others garments.

Education was the main objective in bringing up a family and many sacrifices were made towards this end. The boys were sent to St. Francis Xavier College (StFX) and the girls to Mount St. Bernard Academy, both in Antigonish, Nova Scotia. These institutions were run by the secular priests of the Congregation of Notre Dame. Nova Scotia was noted for a high standard of education.

Mary Ann attended Mount St. Bernard Academy, an all women's college, graduating in 1906. Her godfather was Fr. Ronald MacDonald, a highly respected priest and he assisted in financing her education at Mount St. Bernard Academy.

Mount St. Bernard at StFX students on routine Sunday outing taking a walk through the Antigonish downtown ca 1912.[122] Mary Ann MacDonald attended this prestigious academy.

Mount St. Bernard was the first Catholic women's college in North America to provide courses leading to a bachelor's degree. Students lived on campus under strict supervision. The first women graduated in 1897.

Upon leaving the "Mount", Mary Ann attended the Provincial Normal School in Truro, Nova Scotia, a town she always described as a "pretty town". The Normal School was a teachers training college and Mary Ann graduated in 1907. Her first teaching assignment was in the mining town of Inverness, Nova Scotia. She never forgot her most notorious student, John Joe Develin. He would steal the children's rubbers and try to sell them downtown.

Normal School Truro, Nova Scotia ca. 1915.[123] Opened in 1855, the school was popular for young women in the Maritimes, as the tuition was often subsidized by the provincial government. Mary Ann MacDonald graduated from this teachers college.

In those days teaching consisted not only of teaching, but dressing the students in the winter for their departure at the end of the day. Life was hard due to the extreme poverty in the town of Inverness and the teachers received a starvation salary!

Provincial Normal School Class ca. 1907, in Truro, Nova Scotia.[124] Mary Ann MacDonald is on far left, second row.

The Move Out West

Due to poor health with arthritis, and the poverty in the country side, Mary Ann was advised to consider a new locale. So in the year of 1907 accompanied by her sister, Margaret Agnes, and her brother George Duncan, she set out by train for Western Canada. This was a long trip and trains were most uncomfortable. George, on recounting the trip, tells of the train conductor advising Margaret upon arrival in Montreal, to buy a bottle of brandy for Mary Ann due to her sickness.

They arrived in Winnipeg, where the search for jobs began and the pioneering of the west faced them. Mary Ann and Margaret sought jobs as teachers, and George, who had graduated from St. Francis Xavier

College with a B.A. degree also faced the prospect of teaching, a profession he cared little for.

Mary Ann found herself living in rural areas among immigrants to this country who spoke little English. They comprised of Germans, Polish and in some areas English, who settled on new agricultural lands in an attempt to build homes for their families.

It was the custom for families to board their teachers, one family would take the teacher until Christmas and another family would provide her with room and board for the later half of the teaching year. Often these people did not belong to the same religious persuasion as the teachers, hence, bigotry and lack of privacy were conditions to be tolerated.

The teachers were provided with a horse which Mary Ann rode side-saddled to school. Upon arrival at school it was her duty to light the fire and have the school house warm for classes. As language was a problem, Mary Ann attempted to teach the students English with the aid of T. Eaton's mail order catalogue. She became very intolerant of sunflower seeds as the students used to spit them onto the classroom floor.

School teacher Mary Ann MacDonald with students in Western Canada.[125]

Mary Ann deplored the fact that young girls were allowed to be married at fourteen years of age. Families in those days were hugh, ten and up. Since there was little money to educate children, it became imperative that girls find a husband as soon as possible, and that the young couple become established on another farm where the cycle would be repeated. Usually the home farm went to one of the sons with whom the parents lived until they died.

After teaching in Manitoba under adverse conditions, Mary Ann went to Saskatchewan where she and another teacher, Miss Cameron (also from the Maritimes) taught at Killaly. Here they were provided a teacherage with housing accommodation provided by the school. This was an improvement being situated near the school and having a place of their own in which to live.

It was while teaching in Killaly that Mary Ann met Thomas John Wild who was farming three miles from the village.

The Wild - MacDonald Wedding

On November 27, 1917, Mary Ann and Thomas John Wilde were married in the Immaculate Conception Church in Winnipeg, Manitoba. Only two attendants and a priest were at the wedding; the only family member there was Mary Ann's sister, Margaret Agnes. None of the relatives were advised of the marriage until the couple returned to Killaly. The village of Killaly, like all small places was a very gossipy place.

Thomas John Wild and Mary Ann MacDonald on their wedding day, November 27, 1917.[126]

Life on the farm was a new experience for Mary Ann. Tom had one quarter section of land to farm which meant a considerable amount of work. It was necessary to hire a maid to assist with the housework and sometimes two hired men were required to assist in working the land. Even with hired help, Mary Ann had considerable work to perform; planting a garden, milking cows, making butter, etc.

Thomas John and Mary Ann Wild with baby Kathleen Wilde (author) at Qu'Appelle Valley, Saskatchewan.[127]

Three children were born while living on the farm; Kathleen, John Harold and Ronald Joseph. Mary Ann did not care much for living on the farm; it was extremely lonely and the work was difficult as she had no experience to living on a farm. Besides, at the end of the year, when all expenses had been taken care of, there was barely enough money left for a new dress. She made nearly all the clothes for the children.

The Name Change: "Wild" to "Wilde"

It was also during these times that Mary Ann changed the family's surname from "Wild" to "Wilde" with an "e". The connotations of the name "Wild" had bothered Mary Ann. She knew the surname is derived from a nickname representing "wild, violent, untamed."[128] So she decided to add an "e" to Wild. All family members changed their name to Wilde except, ironically her husband, Thomas, who was set in his ways and kept his last name as Wild. Carl Wild also kept the last name as Wild, along with all of his children. Stanley Wilde changed his name to "Wilde" along with all of his children.

Therefore, all of Mary Ann's children, the four boys and Kathleen, had their last name as "Wilde" and all of their decedents have carried on the surname "Wilde".

Health and Social Activities

In those days, little boys were dressed in white for Sundays and outings. The main social event of the summer was "the picnic". Mary Ann would sew for a whole week before the event, a fruitless task considering how long white clothes stayed clean on little boys.

One advantage that Mary Ann obtained during her life in Western Canada was relief from arthritis. However, as the family became of school age and the school was three miles away, she decided that they had enough of the farm.

The Lumber Business

Tom decided to go into the lumber business. His first assignment as a lumber agent was a place called "JoeVille". It was located in southern Saskatchewan about thirty miles from the US border. The town was in the process of being built; a church, school, etc. It later became known as Lisieux, named after St Thérèse of Lisieux of France, also known as the Little Flower. St. Theresa died at age 24 on Sept 30, 1897. Therese was canonized on May 17, 1925 by Pope Pius XI, only 28 years after her death. A popular saint of the day, the town of JoeVille was proudly named Lisieux after her.

St. Theresa of Lisieux at age 8 (right) with her sister Celine in 1881.[129]

The community was French, the only English speaking families being the Wilde's and the Greenwald's, who were Protestant. Mrs. Greenwald was a large framed lady who was very bossy and a little mean. However her daughter Clara and Kathleen were good friends. Everything at the church was French, although English was taught at the school. One young priest from Quebec came to Lisieux to relieve the parish priest. He was so conscientious, that he felt an English sermon for the only English family in the Church, the Wilde's, was appropriate. As he new no English, this was a formidable task; nevertheless, with Mary Ann's assistance, he struggled with some success to this end.

While residing in Lisieux, a third son, Hugh Gerald, was born to the family.

The French people of Lisieux thought that the man running the lumber yard should be French and requested the lumber company to place a French agent there. This was done and the Wilde's were transferred to Killaly.

The new French agent did not meet with much success in Lisieux as he stole money received for payment of the church and in an attempt to hide the evidence, burnt down the church and rectory.

The family moved to Killaly before the Great Depression of 1929. Economic conditions became progressively worse. Salaries afforded a bare existence and suitable housing in small towns was hard to come by. It was necessary to mortgage the farm which was rented, to support the family. There were no social assistance programs that exist today and eventually the lumber company laid off employees including Tom. Around this time, Ralph Maurice was born in Killaly.

Ralph Maurice Wilde and Hugh Gerald Wilde in front of a Saskatchewan gain elevator.[130]

Finally after a year or so, Tom was given an agency in St. Gregor Saskatchewan. The salary was hardly adequate but poverty was the rule of the day. People were far to proud to ask for relief, the only means of survival for the destitute. It became necessary to find money for educational purposes as the local schools only taught up to Grade XI with the assistance of the Saskatchewan correspondence courses. These courses were excellent. However with Grade XI completed, funds from the farm were used first to send Kathleen to the Ursuline School in Bruno, Saskatchewan and John to St. Peters in Muenster, Saskatchewan to complete Grade XII.

In 1935, the Saskatchewan Farm Loan Board attempted to foreclose on the family farm. As the farm was the original homestead when Mary Ann married Tom Wild, the law required that the wife sign as well as the husband before foreclosures could take place. Mary Ann decided to go to Regina with Tom and refused to sign the farm over. In the years to come the farm was rented out and eventually paid for. As the farm was the only asset held by Tom and as jobs he held provided the only sustenance, he would have been virtually penniless in his old age.

The farm in Saskatchewan was sold when the family moved to Winnipeg and land was purchased at Starbuck, Manitoba. In 1976, Tom sold the farm to the Manitoba New Democratic Party (NDP) government for a mere $50,000 ($630,000 in 2017 dollars). We were advised it was worth much more at that time. However the renter, Ray Mann, could not work it any longer and persuaded Tom to dispose of it as soon as possible.

As a side note, Ronald and Kathleen were advised that the farm was worth more than $50,000, but unknown to us, Tom had already sold the property.

A Saskatchewan wheat field.[131]

Chapter 3. Pioneering Times on the Prairies

I was born in the Melville, Saskatchewan hospital on December 13, 1918 to Mary Ann MacDonald and Thomas John Wild who were living on a farm near the village of Killaly, Saskatchewan.

Melville, Saskatchewan, 3rd Ave and Main Street.[132]

During the family residence on my father's farm, two brothers were born: John Harold, nickname "Hal" and Ronald Joseph.

According to my parents and other relatives, I cried for the first year of my life. This was due to the fact that no milk or other food could be found to agree with me. My parents took me to the St. Boniface Hospital in Manitoba but to no avail. Eventually at the age of one year, I overcame the diet problem and turned into a healthy child.

Melville, Saskatchewan Municipal Hospital 1912.[133] Kathleen Wilde, the author, was born in Melville.

During the first eight years of my life my parents lived on a farm about three miles from Killaly, Saskatchewan, a village practically nonexistent today with a population of only 77 people. Killaly was named after a construction engineer named *Killaley* who worked on the building of the railroad. Killaly was incorporated as a village in 1909.

Life on the farm was a lonesome existence for my mother and us children. There were no other children for us to play with and work was the main occupation for our parents. Both my brothers, John Harold and Ronald Joseph and myself were responsible for planting a garden and milking cows as well as other household chores.

Mother would be overjoyed when Sunday visitors arrived; primarily the MacDonald's from Melville, the Walls from Killaly, the Riders and Lottie Bruch, as I recall. I was excited and overjoyed for the girls that came to visit, like Connie MacDonald. Although older than I was it was always a pleasure to visit with her and Rhonda Wall. Katie and Annie Bruch were closer to my age and I always remembered the pleasant times I spent with them on these occasions.

Mr. and Mrs. W. Rider were my God Parents and every time they came to visit, Mrs. Rider had a little present to bring me, usually a little prayer book. The MacDonald's were John Harold's God Parents. Mr. MacDonald ran the creamery in Melville. Other visitors were Mrs. Lottie Bruch, who were Ronald's God Parents.

Uncle Stanley usually arrived for a visit on Sundays. He was a bachelor, and would drive in his own car, which was an exception for these times.

We loved threshing time at 5:00 pm as there were so many goodies to be consumed. Mother did not enjoy this time as she was burdened to feed the threshing workers including lunch in the afternoon and dinner in the evening.

Outings would consist of picnics in the summertime. Mother would be serving before they went out, making sure that white suites were ready for John and Ronald, as no blue jeans were worn for special occasions in those days.

The Golling Neighbors

Our grandmother, Mrs. Veronica Golling, her husband Frank Golling and their family lived one mile from us. Her family consisted of Katherine "Katie" Golling, Mary Golling, Elizabeth Ethel "Bessie" Golling and Joseph Martin "Joe" Golling. Grandmother did not speak a lot of English, rather she was fluent in German, as she was born and raised in Muzylowice, Austria. (Her story as Veronica Wild is Chapter 1.)

Veronica preferred to wear a shawl rather than a hat and her daughters got very tired of trying to convince her to discard the shawls.

We would visit the Golling's and I remember their well cultivated garden and the poppy cakes they baked. Her house always smelled of peppermints and she had nice flowers in the house. I remember how excited she was when on one occasion at my birthday, she and her husband, Mr. Golling, arrived with birthday presents, one being a broom suitable to my size.

Her husband Frank Golling was fond of children and John and Ronald loved to follow him in the fields when they were a little older. He always sang as he worked the fields, "It Ain't Going to Rain Anymore" and "Barney Google".

One song Mr. Golling sang in the fields with children present, while he worked was, "It Ain't Going to Rain No Mo"[134]

"It Ain't Gonna Rain No Mo'" is a song by Wendell Hall (1896–1969). Hall's 1923 recording was a hit in the US and also in Britain. Carl Sandburg, the writer, suggested that the song goes back at least to the 1870s and includes verses in his American Songbag (1927). By the 1920s many variants were already extant in popular culture.

"It Ain't Going Rain No Mo'" Lyrics:

{Refrain}
It ain't gonna rain no more, no more
It ain't gonna rain no more
How in the heck can I wash my neck
If it ain't gonna rain no more

Oh, a peanut sat on the railroad track
It's heart was all a-flutter
Around the bend came Number Ten
Toot! Toot! Peanut butter

{Refrain}

Oh, my uncle built a chimney
He built it up so high
He had to tear it down again
To let the moon go by!

{Refrain}

Oh, how much wood could a woodchuck chuck
If a woodchuck could chuck wood
If he held a saw in his little paw
A ton of wood he could

{Refrain}

Oh, it isn't going to rain anymore, anymore
It isn't going to rain anymore
The grammar's good, but what a bore

So we'll sing it like before

{Refrain}

A man laid down by the sewer
And by the sewer he died
And at the coroners inquest
They called it "sewercide"

{Refrain}

A rich man rides a taxi
A poor man rides a train
A bum he walks the railroad tracks
And he gets there just the same

Another of Mr. Golling's favourite songs he sang in the fields to the children was "Barney Google" (1923).[135]

Barney Google has been around since June 17, 1919 when it first appeared in a comic strip in the Chicago Herald. Tin Pan Alley came up with a novelty song based on the character in 1923.

"Barney Google" Lyrics:

Who's the most important man this country ever knew?
Who's the man our presidents tell all their troubles to?
No, it isn't Mr. Bryan and it isn't Mr. Hughes;
I'm mighty proud that I'm allowed a chance to introduce:
Barney Google—with the goo, goo, googly eyes,
Barney Google—bet his horse would win the prize;
When the horses ran that day,
Spark Plug ran the other way!
Barney Google—with the goo-goo-googly eyes!

Who's the greatest lover that this country ever knew?
Who's the man that Valentino takes his hat off to?
No, it isn't Douglas Fairbanks that the ladies rave about;
When he arrives, who makes the wives chase all their husbands out?
Barney Google—with the goo-goo-googly eyes,
Barney Google—had a wife three times his size;
She sued Barney for divorce,
Now he's sleeping with his horse!
Barney Google—with the goo-goo-googly eyes!

Following Barney Google "The Goo-Goo Song" (1900), the word "Google" was introduced in 1913 in Vincent Cartwright Vickers' *The Google Book*, a children's book about the Google and the creatures who live in Googleland. This is the term that Larry Page and Sergey Brin had in mind when they named their company Google in 1998. In 2002, when Page set up a scanning device at Google (the company) to test how fast books could be scanned, the first book he scanned was Vickers' *The Google Book.*[136]

Prairie Life

We had a white horse named Captain which was used for the buggy because he was a little slow and steadfast but considered safe. Mother would drive horse and buggy with Captain leading the way to Killaly for groceries.

Our two collie dogs, Rover and Tricksie were our favourite pets. Tricksie was very intelligent and would bring the cows home every day. Rover was a beautiful dog but later got his paw caught in a trap set for coyotes and the paw was frozen and fell off. Rover walked around on his remaining three legs.

Author Kathleen Wilde with her two favourite collie dogs; Tricksie and Rover on the farm in Killaly, Saskatchewan.[137]

As it was time for me to attend school, this presented another problem. There was little revenue to be derived from the farm. After hiring men and a girl to help with chores, Mother said you would be lucky enough to have money for a new dress. Mother taught me the first three grades at home.

Enough was enough of the farm life and in 1926 my father decided to rent the farm and go into the lumber business. He was employed by the Reliance Lumber Company as an agent and we moved to what was called JoeVille (do not know who Joe was), a new French settlement being developed about thirty miles from the United States border.

Lumber business; hauling trees in Saskatchewan. Thomas Wild entered the lumber business in JoeVille, Saskatchewan.[138]

The first school I attended was a little one room school house about one mile from where the village was located. My first day at school was not too enjoyable as I was not familiar with school procedures although I was in Grade three! The teacher, Miss Johnson, with her hair always in a bun, was young and very kind. I walked to school each day with some of the other village children.

One Room School in 1894. Mary Ann MacDonald taught in a one room school house while boarding with student families. The Wild children also attended one room school houses.[139]

In an era when transportation was via walking or horse and with no paved roads, travel was difficult. When hauling grain to elevators with horse and wagon, approximately seven miles was considered to be a convenient distance in order to allow one round trip a day.

One of the village characters was Mrs. Christian, the general merchants wife. She would appear in Church with one of the hats from the store and the next day the hat would be back in the store and she could not understand why the hat did not sell.

In 1916, women were given the right to vote in the Western Provinces. Yet, in 1929, Mrs. Christian, the general merchants wife, would not vote as she did not think women should have a vote.

As the area was predominately French, the people requested that the lumber company provide them with a French agent. As a result, our family was transferred to Killaly, Saskatchewan.

Our move to Killaly brought us back to the vicinity of our Grandmother Veronica Golling. The village now had a three room school which taught up to Grade X. Many of the students were rather tough. I attended this school until I reached Grade IX. At this point I rebelled refusing to go to school and decided I would run away if I was forced to go to school by my parents.

And so I remained at home and studied with the aid of the Saskatchewan correspondence course. As my uncle Stan was teaching at Walnester School, I wrote my exams there and he passed me.

The one room school house was taught by Mr. Murphy. I was allowed to use a desk at this school and study Grade X with the Saskatchewan correspondence course. Grade XI was studied at home with this direction. I completed Grade XI successfully in one year.

Our next move was to St. Gregor Saskatchewan; another small village with little housing accommodations. This was really pioneering in the west during The Great Depression times.

Saskatchewan's shield of arms, assigned by royal warrant of King Edward VII on August 25, 1906.[140] On the gold shield is a red lion, a royal symbol of England. Below are three gold sheaves of wheat which represents agriculture, the principal economy of the province.

It was decided to send me to the Ursula Convent in Bruno, Saskatchewan to take Grade XII. This was a different method of studying. We were up at 6:00 am, attended Mass and retired at 9:00 pm. I did not adjust to this type of study.

Before going to Bruno, Uncle George appeared on a Sunday afternoon. He wondered what I intended to be after completing my studies. The only option appeared to be teaching. He did not think much of that idea as I would only be living in the country and end up on a farm. He suggested I take a business course in Saskatoon.

So I was on my way to business college. Mother spent her last 100 dollars on this course of study. At Marshall Business School, I was studying Gregg shorthand, typing etc. You needed to be a robot to get a job as speed in typing was considered criteria in obtaining a job. No jobs were available in Saskatoon and George's wife Bea suggested I go to Winnipeg where Aunt Margaret was in hopes of me finding work in a larger urban center.

Aunt Margaret was only doing substitute teaching by filling in for teachers who became ill or otherwise incapacitated to teach. She was living in a rooming house and the last thing she needed was me on her doorstep. Mother was very cross at me at going to live there as she thought Aunt Margaret would be very strict. This was the case, however and it paid off.

Summary of the cities I have lived in order:
• Melville, Saskatchewan
• Killaly, Saskatchewan farm
• JoeVille, Saskatchewan
• Lisieux, Saskatchewan
• Killaly, Saskatchewan
• St Gregor Saskatchewan,
• Bruno, Saskatchewan (St. Ursula Academy)
• Englefeld, Saskatchewan (family only)
• Saskatoon, Saskatchewan
• Winnipeg, Manitoba
• Montreal, Quebec
• St. Bruno, Quebec
• Niagara Falls, Ontario (current residence)

John Harold "Hal" Wilde

John Harold "Hal", my brother, was born in Melville, Saskatchewan on October 4, 1921 to Thomas John Wild and Mary Ann MacDonald Wilde who were living on a farm near Killaly, Saskatchewan.

He was baptized in Melville by Father Pander, a Polish priest who objected to the name Harold because he did not think there was a saint by that name. The name John was given to him as he was called after grandfather John Alexander MacDonald. Godparents were Mr. and Mrs. Leo MacDonald of Melville.

When he was five years old our parents left the farm with their three children; Kathleen, John and Ronald to live in JoeVille.

On May 29th, 1916 a mission was established under the name of St-Joseph des Poissons. A Roman Catholic Chapel was built at JoeVille in 1916 or 1917 by Ernest Lamontagne. The first priest was Fr. Rahard. Between 1919 and 1921, a farmer priest, Fr. F.M. Gendron came from his ranch in the region to dispense religious services. The chapel was moved in 1926 to a new location due to the railway construction. The new site was named Lisieux. In 1927 this chapel became the rectory at the new site.

Grand opening of JoeVille Catholic Church in 1922.[141] JoeVille, Saskatchewan later became Lisieux, Saskatchewan.

Thomas Wild first worked as a freight-man for J.W. Redgewick, later working for John Rowan and for the John Deere Company. He was also a member of Melville's First Fire Brigade. With the outbreak of WWI in 1914 the Wild Brothers bought more land and established a drayage (dray) company in Melville to transport goods short distances. The brothers disbanded the company a while later, but Thomas Wild stayed on the farm into the late 1920's where he left the farm to work for Reliance Lumber Company.

Saskatchewan lumber yard operation in winter.

JoeVille consisted of only a general store, a garage and some houses, therefore, the need for a lumber yard as the settlement was expanding with new houses and buildings. During this time the village was renamed Lisieux after Lisieux in France, the home of the Little Flower, St. Therese. This was a predominately French area; only two English families of which the Wild's were one.

When the school was completed, there was a delay in obtaining a teacher, so Mary Ann Wilde was asked to teach for the first half of the term. Mary Ann accepted and although John Harold was only five years old and the age for entering school was six, he was taken to school where he started Grade 1. His sister Kathleen (author), having been taught at home by her mother was in Grade 3. Their younger brother Ronald spent the day at his fathers office. Meanwhile, John succeeded in his school work and continued this arrangement.

The first parish priest was Father Menard. He was preparing the children for first communion and as John was in the class, he was also to receive first communion. One cold winter morning he went to Mass with the other children and returned with the news he had received his first communion. His mother, thinking that he was mistaken, questioned Father Menard about it. Father Menard assured her that yes, he had received communion and that was the way he wanted it to be ... he believed that children being innocent, this was the best time for them to receive first communion. So at five years old, John had received first communion with the priest's blessing and no fanfare. Some years later, John and Ronald were confirmed by Bishop Matthew of Regina and at that time they took a pledge not to drink alcoholic beverages until they were twenty-one years of age. This pleased Mother.

The French people of Lisieux requested a French lumber agent and the Reliance Lumber Company complied with their request. The Wilde's were then moved back to Killaly, about 1930. The French agent who replaced my father, stole the payments made for the church and in an attempt to hide his crime by destroying the records, he burnt the church and the rectory. He was sent to jail and the church was rebuilt. Lisieux is a hamlet now with a population of 15.

During the next fifteen years the Wilde's moved several times; from Killaly to St. Gegor to Englefeld, Saskatchewan. The family eventually moved to Winnipeg where educational facilities were stronger and more convenient.

Religion

My father, Thomas Wild, was a faithful member of the Catholic Church and was on the Board of St. Henry's Roman Catholic Church in Melville for a number of years during the time of Father Kasper and Reverend

Pander. He became a founding member of the Knights of Columbus in Yorkton, Saskatchewan.[142]

Education

Education in rural Saskatchewan for Grades 1-8 took place in schools with one or two rooms depending on the number of children in the area. It was compulsory to send all children to school until they had completed Grade 8 or were fourteen years of age. Grade 8 was the last grade for which exams set by the teachers.

High school consisted of Grades 9 through 12. The Department of Education set the exams for these grades, thus maintaining a uniform standard of education for the province. Few teachers were qualified to teach high school in the rural areas. The normal classroom had 30 students in the eight grades and finances did not permit qualified teachers and more classrooms for the higher grades. To solve this problem, the Department of Education hired qualified teachers to set up correspondence courses for Grades 9 - 11. These were excellent courses; instruction was better than could be devised by individual teachers. The course included assignments which were to be completed by the student and sent to the Department of Education at Regina for correction, as well as queries. The only subjects that were not available were physics and chemistry as no laboratories would be available. If space permitted, students could occupy a desk in the local school. The teacher would watch the students progress in the course and supervise the exams. Grade 11 exams were sent to Regina. If space was not available in the school, students studied at home and went to school to write exams only. Of the three prairie provinces; Alberta, Saskatchewan and Manitoba, it was said that Saskatchewan had the best standard of education.

John completed the first three years of high school by correspondence. Since no instruction was available for Grade 12, he was sent to St. Peters College in Munster Saskatchewan (1938-39). Grade 12 covered more than the first year of university. A major adjustment was required changing from home study to that of college life. This was probably due to the courses not being as structured as the correspondence courses, coupled with the daily schedule of boarding school.

Although people had to deal with a lower standard of living than they do today, there was respect for the law and crime and drugs in schools were non existent.

A view of Lemberg, Saskatchewan in 1913, 18 miles west of Killaly.

John's father, Thomas Wild, was largely self educated having spent only a few months at a school in Lemberg and at a business college in Winnipeg. Education, though, was highly rated in his life and he expressed this as a member of the school board.

It was the aim of John's parents, Thomas and Mary Ann to have all their children complete at least Grade 12. This would give them the advantage of being qualified for higher education, or if this were not possible, it was a good education to start out in the world at that time.

Employment

Jobs were scarce in 1939 and in the autumn of that year help was required to harvest the crops. John went to his grandmother's farm (Veronica Wild Golling) to help with the threshing. This entailed bundle racking which is feeding the grain into the threshing machine; each bundle would weigh 138-155 pounds, also required driving a team of horses.

Threshing scene in Saskatchewan.[143]

In 1939 John went to work for the Reliance Lumber Company at Raymore Saskatchewan. Here he trained as the second man under Mr. McKearon who had served during World War I in the calvary division. His training included the grading of lumber, estimating and balancing the books.

In 1940 John took over the lumber yard at St. Gregor Saskatchewan as his father was transferred to Englefeld, Saskatchewan. It was at about this time that he applied to join the Royal Canadian Mounted Police (RCMP).

Before the Second World War broke out, John ran the lumber yard at Englefeld, Saskatchewan. Dad took responsibility for him. Yet, in 1939, World War II broke out and John later went overseas flying Lancaster's over Germany.

John Harold "Hal" Wilde's Military Life

August 1941 - World War II was in progress and John volunteered to join the Royal Canadian Airforce (RCAF).

November 1941 - Signed up in Edmonton and stayed there for three months. The RCMP called him up, but he had already enlisted.

February 1942 - He was sent to Montreal to become a radio technician at McGill University. This was a course he was not interested in and he transferred to air crew.

February 1943 - Started training at Victoriaville, Quebec in the Initial Training School (ITS), a ground school for air crew. He went to Windsor Mills Quebec Elementary Flying School. His flying instructor was Don Witter from Wisconsin.

February 10, 1943 - Completed training on Tiger Moths (on skis) and soloed. Went to Camp Borden to train on the Harvard training aircraft.

May 4, 1943 - First flight on a Harvard aircraft.

August 1943 - Graduated as a pilot, received his wings.

September 1943 - Went to Summerside, Prince Edward Island astronavigation course for one month.

January 1944 - One months vacation.

February 1944 - Went overseas on the Isle de France ship to Bournemouth, England where he waited to be assigned.

July 1944 to September 1944 - Flew Oxfords (twin engine plane) from Kidlington, England.

September 1944 - Flew Wellingtons (long range bomber) on operations from Feltwell, Norfolk and Ossington, in the UK.
Crew on Operations:
    Navigator - Tom Witting from Kitchener, Ontario
    Bombardier - Hank Mille from Toronto, Ontario
    Wireless operator - Murphy from Montreal, Quebec
    Mid Upper Gunman - Fergusen from Ontario
    Rear gunner - MacDonald from Alberta, was 19 years old and the youngest in the crew
    Flight engineer - unknown

1944 Went to Wombleton, UK to train on Lancaster bombers.

Early 1945 - Flew Lancasters on operations. The Lancaster was named "Tamara".
    Hal's personal information WWII:
    Squadron: Blue Nose #434
    Identification No: R139746
    Commission No: J29540
    Rank: Flight Lieutenant
    Lancaster No: 849T

John Harold "Hal" Wilde was a Bomber Pilot in the RCAF 1941-45
(Oct. 4, 1921 - Jan 10, 2007)[144]

Lancaster Bomber, WWII, the plane John Harold Wilde flew as pilot.[145]

Crew of a Lancaster Bomber in WWII. A similar bomber, the crew named "Tamara"" was flown by Pilot Hal Wilde, RCAF.[146]

The Avro Lancaster is a British four-engined Second World War heavy bomber. It was manufactured in Britain and Canada. It was one of the main heavy bombers of the Royal Canadian Air Force (RCAF) during WWII. The "Lanc", as it was affectionately known, became the most famous and most successful of the night bombers.

September 1945 - Volunteered for the Far East (Japan). Flew Lancaster back to Canada via Azores.

November 1945 - John Harold "Hal" is discharged from the RCAF.

John Harold "Hal" Wilde's Civilian Life

After the war John "Hal" Wilde returned to Canada to become an engineer. He took up engineering at the University of Manitoba. This required covering two years of chemistry and physics in four months. These subjects were not covered in previous years on the farm due to a lack of laboratories in rural areas. Mathematics was substituted instead.

1945 - Spent four months taking two years of physics and chemistry

March 1946 - Entered University of Manitoba in Engineering

May 1949 - Graduated as a civil engineer, having completed four years of study in three years.

September 1949 - Entered University of Michigan at Ann Arbor for Aeronautics Engineering

Spring 1951 - Graduated as an Aeronautical Engineer having completed three semesters at Ann Arbor.

1951 to 1953 - Worked in the aircraft industry

May 1953 - Worked for Union Pump in Battle Creek, Michigan

October 1955 - Married Mary McDougall Porter. Lived in Battle Creek, Michigan where their three daughters were born: Julia Marie, Cynthia Ann and Laura Beth.

March 1963 - Moved to Austin, Texas to work for Tyco Engineering as a chief engineer in R&D. Designed and tested new hydraulic motor pump.

October 1964 - Moved to Houston and returned to Union Pump in sales.

September 1975 - Moved to Brookshire, Texas. Worked two years for Wheatley Pump.

1992 - Returned to Union Pump in Tulsa, Oklahoma

Hal Wilde on military leave in Scotland, exploring his roots.[147]

Chapter 4. The Great Depression and Concurrent Drought

As recalled by John Harold "Hal" Wilde, DOB. Oct. 4, 1921

It is surprising when you look back to the hard times of the depression
and drought of the 1930s, how we as children were isolated and shielded
from the hard knocks and worries that plagued our parents during those
years. As the oldest boy in a family of four boys and one older sister (Kay
b.1918, Myself b.1921, Ron b.1923, Hugh b.1928, Ralph b.1930) I cannot
remember ever thinking that we were poorer or more disadvantaged than
other families.

Kay and I were born while Mother and Dad lived on their farm nine miles
south of Melville, Saskatchewan. In 1926 the farm was leased and Dad
took a job of managing a retail lumber yard in Lisieux, and after the crash
of 1929 to lumber yards in Killaly, St. Gregor and Englefeld; all
Saskatchewan small rural villages that served adjoining farming
communities. The province of Saskatchewan is known world wide for its
rolling prairies and famous for its hard summer wheat crops. Oats and
barley are secondary grain crops. Very little manufacturing is done in the
province which has remained at a population just over one million people
to this day.

My father, Tom came to Saskatchewan from Austria with his widowed mother and two younger brothers, Carl and Stan. His mother married Frank Golling and they had four children, Mary and Katy, both nurses, Bess a teacher and Joe who was the youngest. They lived on a farm about four miles from Killaly which is the farm referred to as my grandparents farm, the Golling farm.

It was there that I spent my high school summers enjoying country life, stooking grain sheaves and later being one of the four threshing crew bundle rack team drivers.

A typical stook of prairie wheat.[148]

In early summer farm activity started with haying. Driving a light team of quick horses as the hay was raked into windrows was enjoyable and much easier than forking it from the hay rack. Some years the yield fell as low as 5-7 bushels per acre, a good yield being 35 to 45 bushels for wheat. Higher yield usually meant higher grades.

A rake pulled by horses was one way of getting the hay gathered.[149]

Men pitching forkfuls of hay onto the hay rack. 1927[150]

The village of Killaly had a population of 103 people. The places of business included the railway station where the agent lived on the premises with his family; also the post office managed by Mr. Fawcett and family. The drayman (freight) Mr. Raskob had a barn and four to six horses and a small grocery store that only carried staples and was operated by the owner without any help.

Near Killaly, Saskatchewan[151]

The highlight of our maturing years was a one room school house with one teacher, Mr. Murphy, who taught all grades from the first through the tenth. Each row of seats represented a grade. Those who took French or Latin were taught by Mrs. Murphy as we collected around the kitchen table in their school teacher's house, next to the school. Mr. Murphy was a strict but fair teacher. Older boys who crossed the line were disciplined at the back of the classroom with a strap cut from a tractor belt. Needless to say the learning curve of discipline was a steep one for all students.

Sport activities consisted mainly of skating and hockey in the winter time; tennis, softball and some baseball in the summer months.

The one cinder based tennis court was shared by all ages including the mothers who had priority on its use up to supper time. I used a book on tennis by Don Budge that had excellent sequence of photos to illustrate the different tennis strokes and credited it with being the reason for my moderate success as a player in my teens. The cinders used for the court were donated by the railroad so it was appropriate that the court was located on railroad property next to the railroad station.

By far, the most popular sporting activity was the national sport of hockey. An RCA radio was the center of our Saturday night attention as we listened to the Toronto Maple Leafs Imperial Oil hockey broadcast narrated from Toronto by the eloquent Foster Hewitt.

Toronto Maple Leafs logo worn on hockey jerseys from 1928-1938[152]

Most of us were skating by the age of five and a hockey stick cut from a willow tree was all we needed to get started on the icy roads and alleys near our homes. Our first pucks were cut from a three and a half inch tree limb. As our shooting got stronger we used magazines, held on with rubber bands, to protect our shins. My first pair of skates were figure skates that had been Mothers. The narrow tight shoe lead to frozen toes on numerous cold days. Later when Dad was able to buy me a pair of hockey skates, I had to learn to stride by using the side of the blade rather than the the point of the figure skate's blade.

John Harold Wilde (l) (author of this chapter) with brother Ron Wilde (r) in front of grain elevator owned by the Saskatchewan Wheat Pool coop.[153]

The end of October was the beginning of the four weeks that it took to build our skating rink. The rink was edged with a twelve inch high board rather than the four foot walls of a hockey rink since funds were very limited. Water came from a big slough two miles from town. After cutting a hole in the ice, buckets were used to fill four barrels on a sleigh pulled by two draft horses. To keep warm in the 10 to 20 Fahrenheit degrees below zero weather we would wear two pair of pants. As the outer pair got wet and immediately froze we were protected from the wind and spilled water. The low rink boards modified our style of playing to the point that stick-handling had to be emphasized in order to keep the puck in bounds.

Caboose pulled by horses.[154]

When we went to play the team in the next small town our travel was in a "caboose" drawn by a team of horses. The caboose was totally enclosed on a sled drawn by two horses. It was heated by a small wood stove and had small sliding windows in the front with slots below for the horses reins. Visibility at night was fairly good when the moon was shining since the fields were white with snow. On moonless nights a lot of reliance was placed on the instinct of the horses to follow the road.

In the winter time the farmers came to town with a team of horses hitched to sleighs that had an open grain box that held about sixty bushels of grain used on a wagon in the summer time. A favorite "sport" in the winter was to take our down-hill sleighs and loop the sleigh's rope through the bracket of the farmer's rear sled runner and enjoy a free ride as he left town. Usually two of us participated, each with our own sleigh, attached to the left and right runner of the farmer's sled. The technique was to run as hard as we could, carrying our sleigh, and then glide into the horse drawn sled's rear runner and hook on. After some distance up to a one half a mile we would release and walk back to town.

One day, things got exciting as a second team of horses pulled up close behind us. The young farmer was having fun with us as he knew we couldn't release with his horses breathing down our necks. He would follow close for a mile or two knowing that we didn't want to walk back that far. About a mile out of town my frayed rope broke and my sleigh slid back between the team of horses following me. A few moments later the back of my sleigh contacted the underside of the farmer's sled pole, carrying me along, with horses' hoofs flying on each side of me as lay face down on my sleigh. The farmer brought his team to a stop and our long walk back gave us time to think over our strategy for the next ride.

Grain Elevator woodcut by Walter J. Phillips ca. 1931. The grain elevator became a symbol of the Canadian Prairies Provinces.[155]

Entertainment in hard times lead to innovating that which we accepted as the normal approach to our leisure. Bows and arrows fit in with our cowboy and Indian days. The bows were made from willow trees, as were the arrows which lacked feathers, and overall the accuracy was more imaginative than real. About the time I was twelve years of age Dad gave me the 22 Remington rifle he had owned when he lived on the farm. This meant a lot to me as enjoyed walking for hours through the country grain farms, particularly in the fall and winter, looking for Hungarian partridges or the odd rabbit. Needless to say this small calibre rifle was not the ideal firearm for partridges but I was happy to have it. The partridge is a tough bird and would take three or four hits before they stopped running in the woods.

One winter day I shot at one silhouetted on a poplar tree limb against the winter sky. He dropped to the ground without a flutter. That night as I plucked him the bullet hole was hard to find until the neck was plucked and the bullet had gone through the neck which was the size of a little finger. That was a lucky shot for the 22 is not that accurate at any range unless it is a special match grade rifle.

Prairie gophers had a bounty of 1 cent so many summer mornings were spent trying to snare them. It takes a lot of patience to wait for the gopher to cautiously stick his nose out of the hole and through the snare's loop. At least it was a leisurely pastime and a good teacher of patience.

The wheat farms of Saskatchewan are geographically unique in that they are laid out in sections of 640 acres, one mile square and further divided into quarters of a section, 160 acres each. This logical layout makes it easy to identify property lines and as such the majority of farms were not fenced. Another reason for the absence of fencing lay in the fact that grain crops and not cattle is the use for this rich soil. Cattle, for the most part, fulfilled the populations dairy and beef needs which were a minimum for this province of 900,000 plus population. With this background it is understandable that farmers did not raise objections to people they knew from crossing their land.

Typical pioneer wheat farm in southern Saskatchewan.[156]

One Saturday morning two of my friends, Vernon McHarg and Harry Murphy and I headed for the country with our 22's and upon coming to a large slough with wild ducks on it decided to see if we could hit one of them. As we laid down on the one bank of the slough the ducks swam toward the six foot bank on the opposite side, the top of the bank being covered with poplar trees and brush. In an hour or so the three of us must have touched off fifty rounds without hitting a single duck. Many of the ducks dove, all kept swimming as though they knew that was the secret to longevity. As the shots ricochetted off the water we could see them hit the bank and while others hit higher in the brush, there impact could not be seen.

Monday morning the farmer, on whose property we had been shooting, asked Dad if I and my friends had been shooting at the slough as he found his one year bull dead with many 22 bullet holes in him. Dad said he would ask me when got home from school and get back with him. Yes, we had been shooting at ducks at the slough but did not see or intentionally shoot at any livestock. Apparently the young bull was in the brush which was heavy enough to conceal him but not heavy enough to stop the 22 shots. Three fathers paid for the young bull and three teenagers were much wiser about shooting off a surface that could cause a ricochet. The confidence in me that Dad showed when he accepted my explanation of this unhappy incident, without so much as showing anger or raising his voice did much to bond the respect and trust that I held for my Dad. Vernon McHarg entered the RCAF about a year before I did and was killed over Cologne while a bomber pilot. Harry Murphy died in a diving accident in a river near Toronto. Only by the Grace of God have I been able to see close to sixty more years than they did.

Newspaper headlines in Saskatchewan report the stock market crash of October 29, 1929. The crash of 1929, combined with drought during the 1930s, would have disastrous consequences for Saskatchewan farmers.[157]

In retrospect it is easy to understand that during the depression the major concern of families was shelter, food and clothing. Add drought and unemployment to the scenario and the picture darkens for any family. Immigrants from Germany in the 1920s were financially set back by the 1929 market crash, unable to make payments on their equipment, they went back to Germany. Unfortunately it was then that Hitler was building his power base that eventually led to World War II. Discouraged for the second time, I am told that some of them returned to Canada.

The plus side of the thirties was that families were physically, socially and religiously closer than families are today. Fifty percent of the population lived on farms that raised grains, dairy products and the foods that fed the general population.

Air transportation was non-existent, cars were not affordable by the average family and when they traveled over the rough gravel roads it was at 30 mph. A distance of fifty miles was a long trip. Dad had bought a 1929 Chevrolet four door sedan which cost $625.00, the only car he ever owned. It was an irony of the times that I earned my wings as an RCAF pilot before I learned to drive a car or even owned a bicycle. I guess you could say that my transportation went from feet to wings.

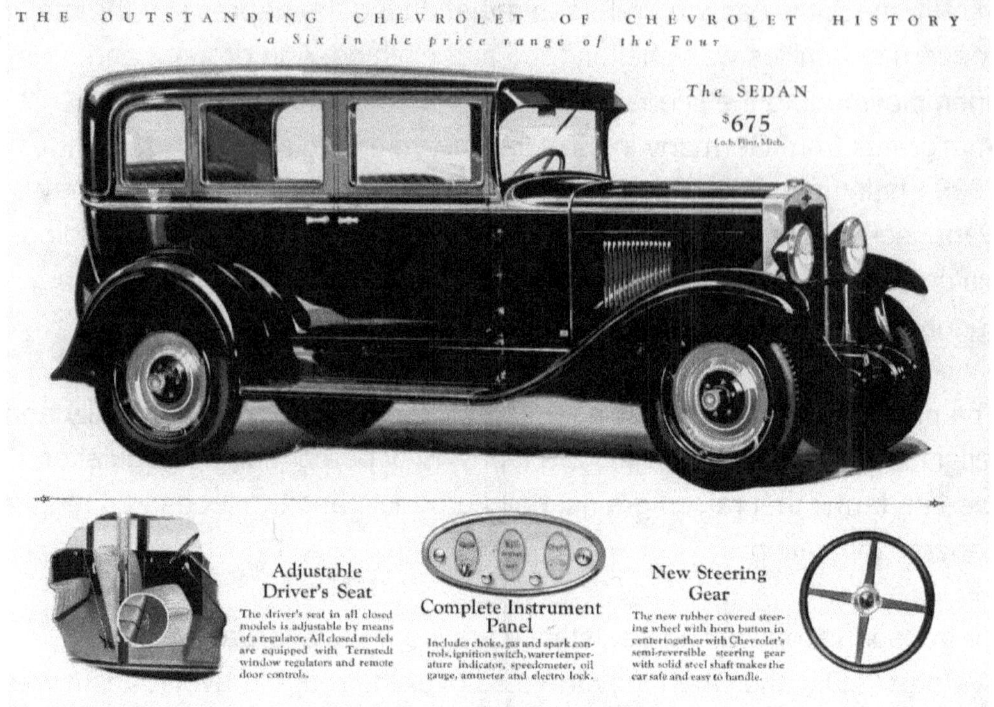

The Wilde's first car, a 1929 Chevrolet four door.

In the small towns and farming communities the depression prolonged the use of horses, which were used for transportation, pulling wagons and buggies in the summer, sleighs and cutters in the winter months. Our mission priest at St. Gregor rode his horse from the town of Englefeld eight miles away, every Sunday. Even when temperatures reached forty degrees below he would be there on time, his horse and clothes covered with frost.

Tractors with lugged wheels were beginning to replace horses on farms in the early thirties. In the larger cities electric street cars were very efficient people movers. The sight of a light ski plane landing on a field near our small town was a big event. The RCMP used a snowmobile, driven by a small aircraft engine with a pusher propeller, to travel without depending on roads.

The dinner table was the culmination of much innovation and expertise on the part of Mother as she succeeded in preparing nourishing meals for our family of seven. Except for excessive fat on meat, I don't recall that any of us turned down any of the food set before us. Our staples were bought from the local grocery. Vegetables were grown in a garden plot a quarter of a mile from home. Water was hauled from a nearby shallow well using our little red wagon. Carrots, beans, cucumbers, beets, tomatoes and rhubarb were the main items grown and later canned for winter use. Mother was the head gardener and chided me for weeding out the carrots as they looked like grass to me. Our potatoes came from a larger plot of land about two miles from home. Dad, Ron and I walked to the potato patch, worked for four or more hours and came home hungry. Seeding, cultivating, spraying the bugs and digging up the potatoes accounted for the balance of the trips to harvest the most important vegetable of our diet.

MacIntosh apples from British Columbia were a winter treat in the fruit category. A crate would be kept in the basement and usually lasted through Christmas. A wild berry, the Saskatoon berry, would be the object of at least one day of picking by the whole family. Very similar to the blueberry, it too was canned for the winter.

Saskatoon berry looks like blueberries but are more closely related to the apple family.[158] Picking this berry was a whole family activity. It was canned for winter use.

When the old brindle cow from our grandparent's farm quit milking she became a menu of tough but tasty steaks for us and the Gollings. Canning meat was a very effective means of preserving meat and a great way of tenderizing it as well. Helping Dad butcher a sheep that we raised was one of the hardest chores I ever had to do as a youngster.

A favorite winter food was fish, both pike and white fish. The pike were bought for two cents a pound, the white fish for three cents. The fish were packed in snow and stored on the verandah for the rest of the winter.

Heating a house was a major undertaking, especially on a low budget. Our home was heated by a wood burning Round Oak stove while cooking was done on another wood-burning stove, a four-burner that also served as a heater on cold winter nights. Coal was too expensive to use. The wood was poplar, hauled in from the Indian Reservation on a sled drawn by a small underfed team of horses. The trees were about twenty-five feet long and represented approximately one and a half cords, the price we paid being $1.75 for the load. Traveling from the Qu'Appelle Valley, seeing the Indian with his squaw and a little one wrapped in heavy blankets was a common sight. Mother had a big meal cooked for them before they set out on the long trip home. Ron and I had the job each day of cutting and splitting the wood for the next day. Since poplar is a soft wood, Dad would stay up until 1:00 a.m. on winter nights to keep the Round Oak stove burning, while Mother got up at 6:00 a.m. to restart the fires. Such was the marathon of self-preservation on typical cold winter nights that could get as low as forty degrees Fahrenheit below and sometimes colder.

(l-r) Ron Wilde, Ralph Wilde, Thomas John Wild, Hugh Wilde, Hal Wilde in front of Saskatchewan Wheat Pool grain elevator.[159]

When you are brought up in cold weather country you soon learn to appreciate the value of wool in clothing to fight off the freezing temperatures. Wool has a wicking action that pulls moisture from the surface of your skin and in so doing keeps your skin dry. At the same time the cellular nature of the yarn acts as a good insulator and cushion. A moist wool sock will still keep your foot warm; a wet cotton sock is a disaster to a cold foot. In addition to her other homemaker talents, Mother would knit mittens, socks, scarfs and toques for us. A foot pedal Singer sewing machine was kept busy as she made shirts and even blue jeans from yard goods bought through the Eatons or Simpson mail order catalogue. Our wood floors were covered with rugs that were braided from cut up old clothes and worn blankets. Hooked rugs were the smaller and fancier rugs that I recall Mother working on in the evenings.

Kerosene mantle lamps were used as we did not have any electricity. The other challenge was not having any plumbing and that meant using the famous outdoor house. When new holes had to be dug, I recall they were about eight feet deep to get below the frost line. Being constipated was almost preferable to going outside on a cold winter night.

Since Grade 10 was the highest grade in our one-room school house I studied Grade 11 at home by correspondence. My powers of concentration must still have been in the developing stage for it took me two years to complete the eleventh grade. Kay was a better correspondence student and only required one year. Mother and Dad recognized my handicap and raised enough money to send me to St. Peters College at Muenster, Saskatchewan for my twelfth grade. My friends Harry Murphy and Vernon McHarg attended the same year and since I had an early start at first grade I was still able to finish high school at the age of seventeen. This was the last summer that I spent on my grandparent's farm. Shortly after that I was asked by Dad's lumber yard superintendent if I would go to Raymore as a "second" man for a few months since their man had fallen off a platform and broken a leg. My qualifications were respectable for Dad had taught me how to pile lumber, know the grades and types of wood and moldings, plus how to balance the sales and inventory ledgers. I don't remember discussing wages since having a job was more important than what you earned in depression years.

My wages at Raymore were thirty dollars a month. Twenty-five dollars went for my room and meals at the Raymore Hotel which was a bargain. Spending the five dollars that was left over wasn't hard to do but even then a couple of dollars were saved. The manager at Raymore was a World War I cavalry veteran with many interesting stories to tell about his overseas service. In all, a pleasant atmosphere for my first job out of high school.

The second surprise came a few months later when I was asked to run Dad's St. Gregor yard since he was being transferred to Englefeld. My wages didn't change but room and board dropped since housing was provided. This job lasted almost two years to November 1941 at which time I reported to the RCAF in Edmonton. My acceptance into the RCMP came three days later (three days too late) for I had also applied for enlistment with them almost two years earlier. For me the depression days had come to a close and a new turn in life opened up with many Graces from God that have been my good fortune.

When Dad was told that there was a book out on the Depression he replied that he didn't have to read it, he had lived it. And so to my recollection of those days makes me aware that I was brought up during the Depression without realizing the significance of that era, or understanding at the time, the burdens it placed on my parents.

A monument to their dedication in bringing their five children through the 1930s, is the knowledge that all of us received our college degrees by working our way through our education objectives without help that they would have liked to have given us.

- John Harold "Hal" Wilde

Wilde Family Portrait.

(l-r) Hugh Gerald Wilde, Ronald Joseph Wilde, Mary Ann Wilde, Thomas John Wild, Kathleen Wilde, John Harold "Hal" Wilde and Ralph Maurice Wilde. This photo after Mary Ann added the "e" to the end of "Wild" making the surname "Wilde". Thomas and his brother Stanley kept their given surname, "Wild". Their brother Carl, changed his surname to "Wilde".[160]

Acknowledgments

I wish to thank my nephew, Brian Wilde for his assistance, without which this book would never have gone to press.

A special thanks to John "Hal" Wilde who had the foresight to write his story (Chapter 4) so future generations could benefit.

I'd also like to thank Brian J. Lenius who contributed to research on our European ancestors.

Many thanks to Cathy Wilde Patapis who assisted me identifying our family photo collection.

Appendix

I. How the Brick Wall Came Down

A brick wall prevents you from uncovering the records or whereabouts of an ancestor. In the Wild genealogy discovery, not knowing Franz Wild's ancestral village prevented us from learning more about his life, his parents and siblings. Aunt Kay (Kathleen Wilde) narrowed his hometown to somewhere near Lemberg and Grodek. She also had a photo of Franz in military uniform from family records. She was very close to locating Franz's hometown.

Here is how the breakthrough came in locating Franz Wild's records:

In August 2017, we had a communique with Dick Mann from British Columbia. The Mann's and Wild's share a family link; Stanley Wild married Rose Mann. In discussing our dilemma in an email dialogue, Dick provided a map of several dozen German colonies in Galicia. Unbeknownst to us, one of the colonies is where Franz Wild had lived. Yet we were unable to crack the brick wall.

The Church of the Latter Day Saints (LDS) Family Search Center in Reading PA, was able to provide the Hamburg-Amerika Line passenger list with Veronica Wild's entry record.

Nicole Watier, a Genealogy Consultant with Library and Archives Canada, also provided the passenger list for Veronica Wild from the Montreal Quebec arrival entry. Nicole referenced the East European Genealogical Society based in Manitoba as an organization knowledgeable in this area.

The Hamburg-Amerika Line departure passenger list shows Veronica Wild and her three boys entry on the voyage and her residence as

"Narodowe". She was from a small village and would have thought everyone would have known Narodowe. This was a clue, but Narodowe, as a standalone village name in Galicia, did not surface.

In October 2017, Shannon Dittrick - LePage, who has extensive family trees on MyHeritage and Ancestry.com, identified Veronica's stated village of "Narodowe" on the Hamburg passenger list, as Muzylowice Narodowe. Shannon had previously researched the Kleczko family and kindly provided Veronica Kleczko's birth record in Muzylowice. Yet, she had no details on Franz Wild.

Subsequently, around this time, the East European Genealogical Society was contacted and Brian J. Lenius, a professional genealogist responded. Brian, an expert in Galicia, has been to the village of Muzylowice over twenty times over the years. His family lineage is also from Muzylowice and the Wilde family share common ancestors with Brian's family - Joseph Schnerch and Jakobina Jestadt. Brian researched his extensive collection of resources and supplied numerous documents of births, marriages, and deaths pertaining to the Wild and Kleczko families. To light, came the life records of Franz Wild; his birth, marriage to Veronica, his siblings, cause of death, the Wild family lineage for three generations and a history of this small village. Aunt Kay called this finding a miracle.

Also, in 2004, Brian J. Lenius teamed up with Edward Rozylowicz and others to fundraise and erect in Muzylowice a large monument in the German Roman Catholic cemetery as a memorial to the colonists buried there. The Wild, Kleczko and Schnerch names are among forty colonist surnames on the monument.

Franz Wild had been found and the brick wall came down!
- Brian Wilde

II. Details of Muzylowice Genealogy Resources

There are no surviving birth registers or bishop copies of births from the beginning of the colony until 1826 in the Muzylowice Roman Catholic Parish. The bishop copies of birth, marriage and deaths exit from 1826 up to about 1900. If there were earlier bishop copies prior to 1826 back to the beginning of the colony they do not exist.

Regarding the original parish register books, the first two parish register books of births, titled Liber Natorum, from ca. 1784 to 1845 are missing. The first marriage register book, titled Liber Copulatorum, from ca. 1784 to 1830 is also missing. Two books of original parish death registers, titled Liber Mortuorum start in 1787 and end in 1882. We rely on the bishop copies for births from 1826 to 1845 and marriages from 1826 to 1830. To augment these vital register books I also have accumulated official birth "certificates" made out by the Muzylowice parish priest for births, marriages and deaths. This fills in a few of the earlier missing records prior to 1826. Some of the certificates are relevant for the Wild genealogy and available upon request.

There are also two books of *Liber Status Animarum*. These are unique books that were kept by parish priests to identify all parishioners that lived in each house in the parish. Normally, it only includes the houses of Roman Catholics if it is an R.C. book. Not many of these books survived. In fact, there are none surviving for most parishes. But we are fortunate that we actually have two such books for Muzylowice. I found one in the state archive in Krakow and another in the state archive in Warsaw.

These books have a separate page for each house and are like family group sheets, or several group sheets on one page. It is not like parish register books that record births, marriages, and deaths with each record representing a single event. Instead the Status Animarum is a compilation of all information at the time drawn from the parish registers pertaining to each family. New events (births, marriages, and deaths) are added as they occur and people are stroked out when they die or move away. This can lead to a very messy and cluttered page, but all the information on one page can be a goldmine.

There are other sources as well for Muzylowice, including cadastral land records that are associated with property maps from 1853 and 1883. We have land records from 1788, 1820, 1853, 1879, and 1883. We also have three versions of cadastral maps created at the same time as the 1853 land records. These maps and land records give the landowner / head of household, but they do not give relationships (parents or children) and don't give birth, marriage or death information. However, it is possible to locate where the family lived in the village, who the neighbors were, etc. It nicely fleshes out a "family history."
- Brian J. Lenius

III. Naming Canadian Cities after European Cities

Lemberg (today it is L'viv, Ukraine) gave its name to Lemberg, Saskatchewan and is also a sister city to Winnipeg. Neudorf in German means "New Village" and so it was a very common place name in German-speaking areas of Europe. Neudorf, Saskatchewan was named after a village in Europe, but we can't be sure which one because there were literally hundreds if not thousands of places with this name. However, there were three places with this name in Galicia where most of the settlers in the Lemberg-Neudorf area of Saskatchewan came from.
- Brian J. Lenius

Austro-Hungarian City	Austro-Hungarian Province	Country (1890)	Current Name	Other names	Canadian Sister City
Muzylowice Narodowe - - - - - - Muzylowice Koolina	Galicia	Austro-Hungarian	Muzhylovychi Lviv Oblast, Ukraine	Muzylowice: Polish Muzhylovychi: Ukraine Münchenthal: German	none
Lemberg	Galicia / Galizien	Austria Hungary	L'viv, Ukraine	L'vov; Russian Lwow: Polish Lemberg: German	Lemberg, Sask Winnipeg, Manitoba
Neudorf	Galicia	Austria Hungary	Neudorf, Ukraine		Neudorf, Sask
Gródek Jagielloński	Galicia	Austria Hungary	Horodok, Ukraine		none
Chernivtsi	Bukovina	Austria Hungary	Chernivtsi, Ukraine		Saskatoon, Sask

IV. The Wilde Ethnicity Explained

If you are an American citizen your nationality is American. If you are a Canadian citizen you are Canadian. We don't have a "European nationality" unless we have citizenship in a country in Europe. Having said that, my ethnicity includes German, but on my mother's side, my ethnicity is Irish and Scottish. The ethnicity on the Wild side is both German (Wild, Schnerch, Jestadt) and Polish (Kleczko). Kleczko is a Polish name, not German. For example, you could say that you are of German and Polish ethnicity (or heritage) and Austrian nationality because they lived in Galicia within the Austro-Hungarian Empire.

- Brian J. Lenius

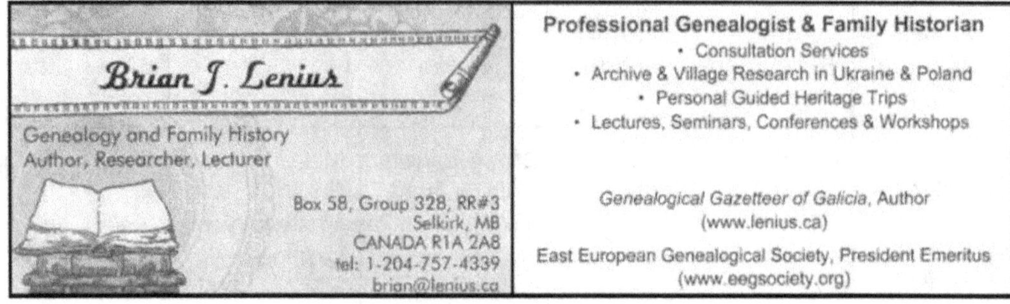

V. East European Genealogy Society (EEGS)

Brian J. Lenius, who contributed much of the European materials for this Wilde family history book is President Emeritus, and was co-founder of the EEGS genealogical society. He remains an active member today.

This Society is useful for those pursuing their personal genealogy and would like to network with others that are researching in the area of East Europe including Galicia, Bohemia, Bukovina, Volhynia, Germany, Austria, Ukraine and Poland. The society's "Research Consultants" provide one-on-one assistance to help members move forward with their research. The Society has about 400 members world-wide. About 1/3 of the members are in Manitoba, 1/3, in the rest of Canada, and 1/3 in the USA with a few in Britain, Australia and Germany. Members receive a quarterly internationally recognized journal; *East European Genealogist,* as part of their membership. The society contact information is:

East European Genealogical Society
P.O. Box 2536
Winnipeg, MB
CANADA R3C 4A7
www.eegsociety.org
info@eegsociety.org

VI. Current Village of Muzylowice

Village of Muzylowice, home to three generations of Wild's.[161]

Typical farmstead in the Village of Muzylowice/Münchenthal.[162]

VII. The Münchenthal German Catholic Cemetery Memorial

The German Catholic Cemetery Memorial Monument is a memorial to the German colonists buried in the Münchenthal Roman Catholic Cemetery which is the current day village of Muzhylovychi, Ukraine. Included in the cemetery are the Wild family, Kleczko family, and Schnerch family, among others. All these families are part of our heritage.

The memorial monument will be blessed on September 20, 2018 with a special ceremony conducted by a local Roman Catholic priest. All descendants of families buried in the cemetery are welcome to attend. It promises to be a very moving day and will be a reunion with the coming together of our families in the village for the first time in over 70 years. For information please contact Brian J. Lenius at brian@lenius.ca

In 2004, two descendants of Münchenthal families, Brian J. Lenius and Edward F. Rozylowicz decided to start a project to restore this cemetery in our ancestral village. A tremendous amount of time was taken to fundraise, plan, organize the work, and see it to completion. Initially, it was not even possible to find the cemetery in the village unless a person knew exactly where it was. It was an overgrown dense thicket of trees and shrubs. Now after nearly 15 years of work and maintenance, the cemetery is recognizable and has a large monument in the centre as a memorial to the German Colonists buried in the cemetery.

- Brian J. Lenius

A view of the current cemetery and the German Catholic Cemetery Memorial Monument.[163]

The cemetery is about the size of a football field and is surrounded on all sides by a border of trees and woods. The photo above shows the monument in the centre of the cemetery, approximately half way to the far end, where a few original and broken tombstones can be seen.

The monument is approximately 14 feet (4 meters) in height and sits on top of a slightly raised mound.[164]

Memorial detail: shows one of the two black panels engraved with the German surnames of people buried in the cemetery including Wild and Schnerch surnames.[165]

Memorial detail: shows the black panel engraved with the Polish surnames of people buried in the cemetery. Note: Veronica's maiden name of Kleczko is on the panel.[166]

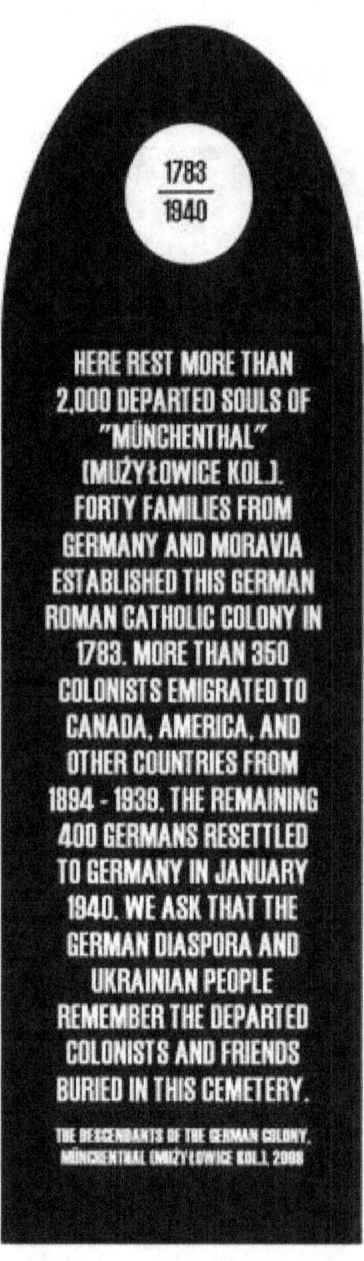

The wording and design graphic for this stone panel briefly sketches the history of the German Catholic colony of Münchenthal. It was created by Brian J. Lenius and Edward F. Rozylowicz. The actual panel on the monument is virtually identical.[167]

VIII. Münchenthal Roman Catholic Church

The Münchenthal Roman Catholic Church, also called the Muzylowice Roman Catholic Church, is where the Wild family were parishioners for three generations. This building in the village was built in 1849, using bricks from the former Jesuit monastery on the site.[168]

All churches were closed down by the Soviets after WWII. There were no Roman Catholics left as they were repatriated during the war. The Roman Catholic church building was burned by the UPA (Ukrainian Insurgent Army) during the war. The fire destroyed the bell tower and burned the roof. Later, the Soviet authorities put a low pitch roof on the building, bricked up the windows, including the large circular window above the entrance. The building was used to store grain and fertilizer for the collective farm. The low pitch roof and bricked windows took away the appearance of the building looking like a church. Since 1999, the roof has fallen in, and with daylight inside, the fertilizer residue has made the trees grow tremendously thick and fast inside. The fertilizer also rotted the brick walls. One wall (right side wall from the entrance) has partially collapsed. Many of the bricks, inside and out, are deteriorated and now have the consistency of chalk.

- Brian J. Lenius

Today, in Muzhylovychi, Ukraine, the church building stands in ruin.[169]

IX. Killaly Roman Catholic Churches and Cemeteries

Mariahilf Roman Catholic Chapel and Cemetery, a Canadian historic site built in 1900, is near the villages of Neudorf and Killaly.[170]

In Lemberg is Saint Michaels Roman Catholic Cemetery where several members of the Wild family are laid to rest. St. Elizabeth Roman Catholic Cemetery in Killaly is where Veronica Wild Golling and Frank Golling are laid to rest.

A brief history of St. Elizabeth Parish:

>The origin of St. Elizabeth's Parish in Killaly, Saskatchewan dates back to the year of 1892.

>Mr. Johann M. Bruch left his native village of Bonndorf near Lemberg, Galicia early in 1892 to verify the prospects advertised in the Old Country regarding the acquisition of land on the Western Prairies. Soon he was on his way back home to move his wife and family to their new homestead. His nephew Konrad Kletschko, joined the family group. On June 22, 1892, they moved from Grenfell to the selected homestead on Sw. 34, Tp. 19, R. 7, W. of

2, two miles west and ~2 mile south of Mariahilf Church. This land
is now owned by Dennis Waldbauer of Neudorf.

In 1893 Mr. Johann Hubenig from Rosch near Czernowitz
(Bukowina) and Mr. Johann Kletschko, father of Konrad, with their
families followed. They found temporary shelter on the homestead
of Johann Bruch, the patriarch of the Catholic settlement that was
to become known as "Mariahilf." With the advent of the C.P.R. line
going through the district, this developed into the Killaly Parish.

In 1895 Father Woodcutter (ed. anglicized?) and Father J. E.
Zerbach, diocesan priests from the Mission of Kaposvar celebrated
monthly masses in the homes of Mr. Johann Bruch, Mr. Anton
Exner and others.

In 1899 the Catholic population of Mariahilf or what is now known
as St. Elizabeth's Parish had increased to such an extent that it
warranted the visit of Archbishop Adelard Langevin of St. Boniface
to administer the sacrament of Confirmation to fifty-four young men
and women. This important event took place on the Bruch farm on
May 8, 1899.

In 1900 the Mariahilf Church was built six miles south of the
present village of Killaly by Fr. P. J. DeBresson, O. Praem. After
the turn of the century the Oblate Fathers from Winnipeg, Fr. Albert
Kulawy and Fr. August Suffa, took turns in ministering at Mariahilf.
They were followed by Fr. Marcus Kasper.

In 1907 an Oblate Community was established in Grayson to care
for the whole area. In 1921 the Mariahilf Church was destroyed by
fire. The second chapel was built in 1926 which still stands today,
not so much to be used henceforth as a place for divine worship,
but as a reminder of the faith so cherished by the forefathers.

In 1910 the Catholic people began to build a church in the village
of Killaly. Before the work was finished, a storm swept through
leaving the church in ruins. This did not deter the people from
attaining their objective.

The church was dedicated to St. Elizabeth and both churches of the district: Killaly and Mariahilf, were served by the Oblates of Grayson. It was Fr. Kasper from Grayson who looked after these two places until 1911. He was followed by Father Edward Hess, who served until 1915. Following Father Hess came Father Francis X. Rapp, who served until 1925; Father James Schnerch, who served until 1926 and finally Father Anton Bergmann, until the fall of 1929.

In 1929 Father P. J. Schwebius, O.M.I. (1929 - 1933) took up residence at Lemberg and served Killaly from there. His successor Father Joseph Schulte, O.M.I. (1933 - 1935) resided part-time in both Lemberg and Killaly.

In September 1935, Father J. Fuchs, O.M.I., took up permanent residence in Killaly in a rented house. Lemberg now remained a mission to Killaly until appointment of a resident priest in 1939. In the years of 1936 1944 under the direction of Father Fuchs, O.M.I., the parishioners of Killaly started a Rosenkranz (Rosary Society), which formed the ground work of the present St. Elizabeth Society.

Father Joseph Riedinger, O.M.I. (1944 - 1951), succeeded Father Fuchs and in 1945 - 1947 built a larger church which was blessed by Archbishop M. C. O'Neill on July 3, 1948.

- William Thiele[171]

X. DNA Tests Results

AncestryDNA lab service was contracted for the Wild ancestry. AncestryDNA provided ethnicity estimates they say go back 1000 years and genetic community estimates from hundreds of years ago.[172] DNA test results for Kathleen Wilde's nephew follow:

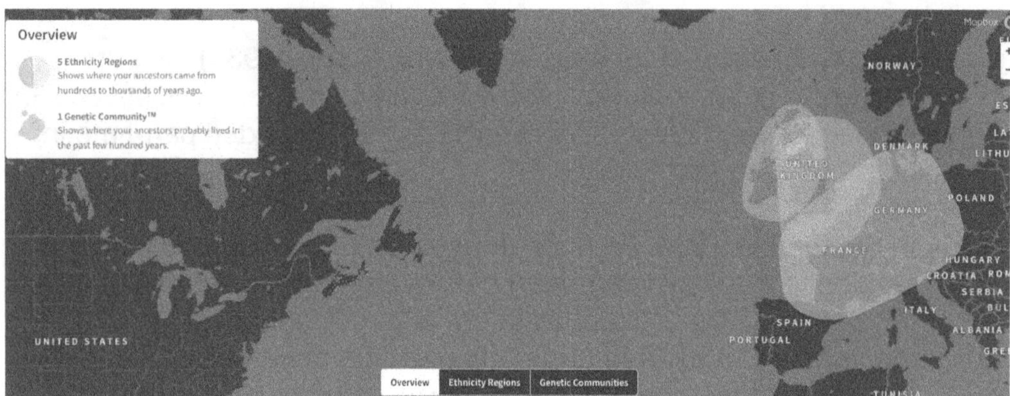

This is an overview map showing the European concentrations.

Genetic community detail highlighting Scotts results.

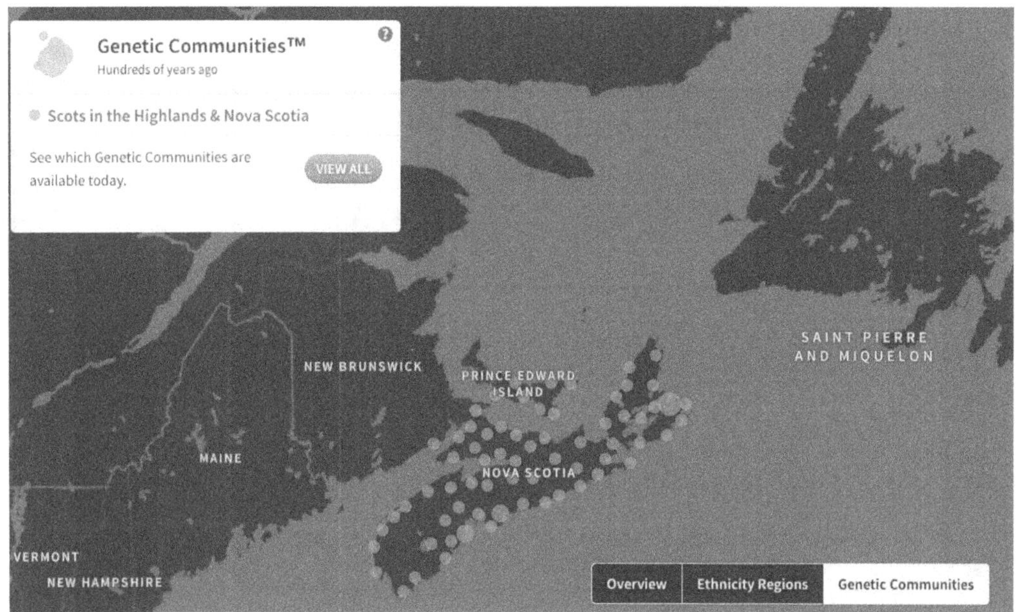

A genetic detail map highlighting Nova Scotia results.

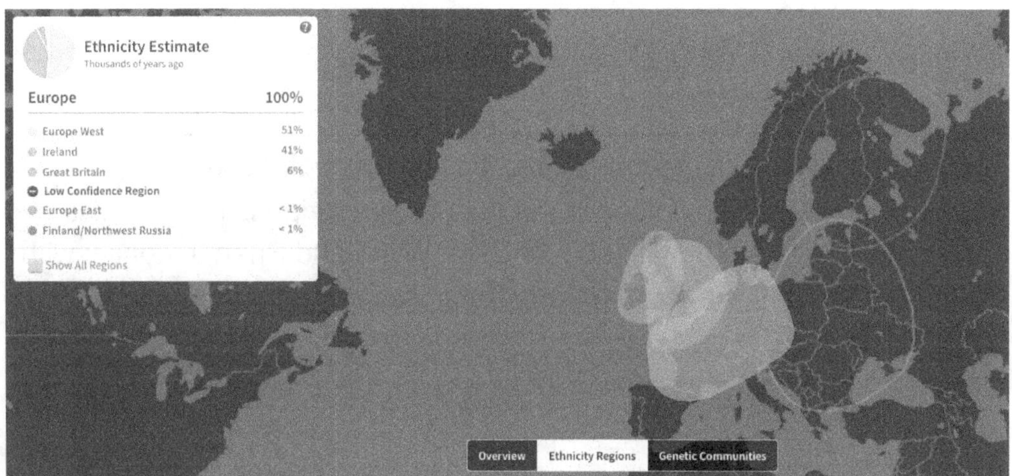

Ethnicity detail Europe; Germany, Ireland, Great Britain (Thousands of years ago)

Note on Ethnicity Estimate: Europe West is primarily located in: Belgium, France, Germany, Netherlands, Switzerland, Luxembourg, Liechtenstein. Ireland is primarily located in: Ireland, Wales, Scotland.

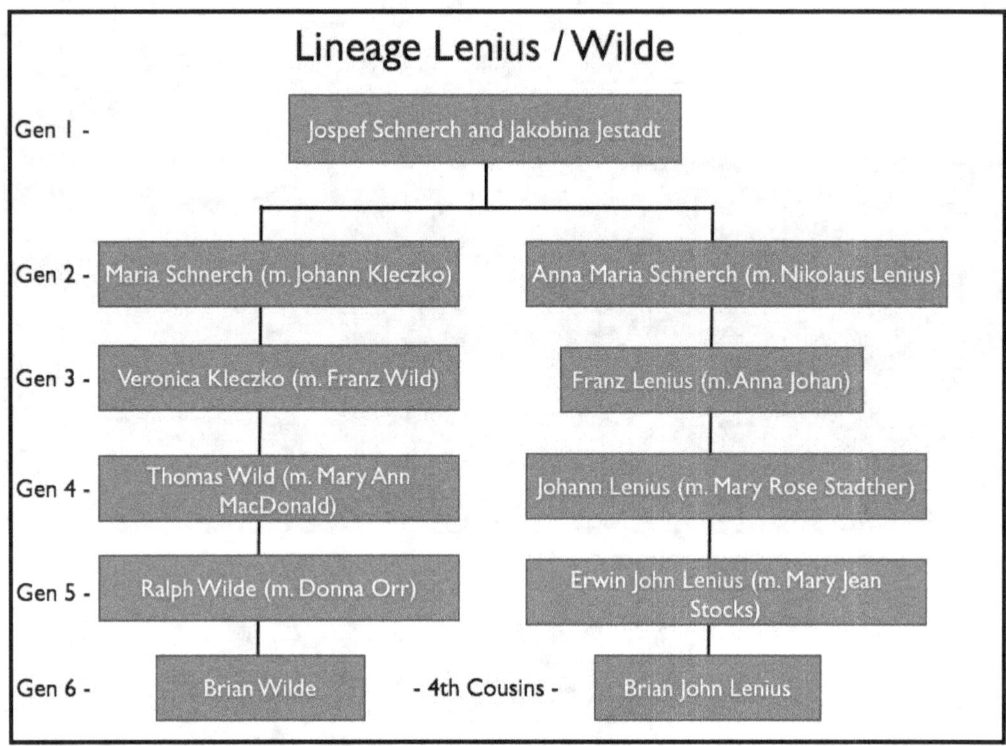

This chart shows the Lenius and Wild ancestors originating from Muzylowice, a German colony in the Austro-Hungarian Empire. It also shows the 4th cousin relationship of Brian Wilde and Brian J. Lenius with the shared great great great grandparents; Joseph Schnerch and Jakobina Jestadt.[173]

XII. Franz Wild Siblings at Time of His Wedding

This chart highlights the Wild family ages, marital status and attendance at the time of Franz Wild's wedding.[174]

NAME	BIRTH	AT TIME OF WEDDING	INFORMATION	ATTENDED WEDDING
Johann Wild	b. 10-Apr-1850 in Münchenthal	d. 27-Dec-1864 in Münchenthal		No
Josef Wild	b. 13-Dec-1852 in Münchenthal	m. 3-Jun-1873 in Ebenau	Married to Marianna **Lenius**. They had 5 children, including an infant at the time of the wedding. This family later immigrated to Canada.	Likely
Anna Elisabeth Wild	b. 27-Jan-1856 in Münchenthal	m. [record not found]	Elisabeth Wild was married to Anton **Kornel** (brother to Thomas) and had had 8 between 1876-1890. Three living children could have attended the wedding with their parents.	Likely
Katharina Wild	b. 24-Jan-1859 in Münchenthal	m. 17-Aug-1875 in Münchenthal	Married to Thomas **Kornel**. They had 6 children, including an infant at the time of the wedding. Thomas was a witness to the marriage.	Yes
Franz Wild (GROOM)	b. 10-May-1861 in Münchenthal	m. 16-Feb-1886 in Münchenthal		Yes
Apolonia Wild	b. 12-Nov-1863 in Münchenthal	m. 15-Jan-1882 in Münchenthal	Married to George **Runge**. Living in the nearby hamlet of Czarnokonce that belonged to the Muzylowice R.C. parish. This family later immigrated to Canada.	Likely
Eva Wild	b. 30-Aug-1866 in Münchenthal	m. not married at time of wedding	Eva was not yet married at the time of the wedding. She married Philip **Runge** the year following this wedding (m. 9-May-1887 in Münchenthal). This family later immigrated to Canada.	Likely
Thomas Wild	b. 02-Jan-1869 in Münchenthal	m. not married at time of wedding	Thomas was not yet married at the time of the wedding. He married Eva **Wittmann** six years later (m. 23-May-1892 in Münchenthal)	Likely

<u>Note</u>: **Anna Elisabeth Wild**, b.27-Jan-1856, is only referred to as Elisabeth in the records for the birth of all her children. It is a common German practice to drop the name Anna or Johann when there is a middle name. For example, Anna Elisabeth Wild became simply Elisabeth Wild. Johann Adam Lenius became simply Adam Lenius for my earliest Lenius ancestor who immigrated to Galicia.

Marianna Lenius was baptized Marianna, but is Maria in her marriage record and for 6 of her children's births. She is Marianna for 2 childrens' births and child's birth simply has Anna. The name Marianna is often shortened to either Maria, Anna or simply kept as Marianna. In this case, the variability throughout the records indicates that we should use Marianna.

Endnotes

Chapter 1

[1] Hobbs, Karen. "Recruiting Rules of The Austrian Army." *East European Genealogist.* Vol. 11, No. 2 (Winter 2002). pp. 6-24. Information provided by Brian J. Lenius

[2] Muzylowice Roman Catholic Parish. Liber Natorum 1845-1887. p.82, no.1861-10. Microfilm GSU_2380055, item 1. Archiwum Glowne akt Dawnych (Zespol 437, Sygnatura 30). Warsaw, Poland. Microfilm image obtained from Brian J. Lenius for the birth of Franz Wild, 10-May-1861.

[3] Ibid.

[4] Ibid.

[5] Muzylowice Roman Catholic Parish. *Liber Natorum 1845-1887.* p.121, 1868-16. Microfilm GSU_2380055, item 1. *Archiwum Glowne akt Dawnych* (Zespol 301, Sygnatura 30). Warsaw, Poland. Microfilm image obtained from Shannon Dittrick Lepage for the birth of Veronica Kleczko, 02-Jul-1868.

[6] Ibid.

[7] Lenius, Brian J. Personal communication. "Citations and Notes" file.

[8] Muzylowice Roman Catholic Parish. *Copiae Copulatorum 1826-1900.* no.1886-2. Archiwum Archidecezjalne w Przemyśl. Przemysl, Poland. Bishop's copy transcribed by Anna and Maciej Orzechowski for the marriage of Franz Wild and Veronica Kleczka, 16-Feb-1886. Obtained from Brian J. Lenius.

[9] Ibid.

[10] Muzylowice Roman Catholic Parish. *Liber Mortuorum 1848-1882.* p.54, no.1864-10. Microfilm GSU_2380055, item 2. *Archiwum Glowne akt Dawnych* (Zespol 437, Sygnatura 32). Warsaw, Poland. Microfilm image obtained from Brian J. Lenius for the death of Johann Wild, 27-Dec-1864.

[11] Muzylowice Roman Catholic Parish. *Liber Natorum 1845-1887.* p.33, 1852-13. Microfilm GSU_2380055, item 1. *Archiwum Glowne akt Dawnych* (Zespol 437, Sygnatura 30). Warsaw, Poland. Microfilm image obtained from Brian J. Lenius of the birth of Josef Wild, 13-Dec-1852.

[12] Muzylowice Roman Catholic Parish. *Liber Natorum 1845-1887.* p.43, 1856-4. Microfilm GSU_2380055, item 1. *Archiwum Glowne akt Dawnych* (Zespol 437, Sygnatura 30). Warsaw, Poland. Microfilm image obtained from Brian J. Lenius of the birth of Anna Elizabeth Wild,27-Jan-1856.

[13] Muzylowice Roman Catholic Parish. *Liber Natorum 1845-1887.* p.61, 1859-2. Microfilm GSU_2380055, item 1. *Archiwum Glowne akt Dawnych* (Zespol 437, Sygnatura 30). Warsaw, Poland. Microfilm image obtained from Brian J. Lenius of the birth of Katharina Wild, 24-Jan-1859.

[14] Muzylowice Roman Catholic Parish. *Liber Natorum 1845-1887.* p.82, no.1861-10. Microfilm GSU_2380055, item 1. *Archiwum Glowne akt Dawnych* (Zespol 437, Sygnatura 30). Warsaw, Poland. Microfilm image obtained from Brian J. Lenius for the birth of Franz Wild, 10-May-1861.

[15] Muzylowice Roman Catholic Parish. *Liber Natorum 1845-1887.* p.99, 1863-19. Microfilm GSU_2380055, item 1. *Archiwum Glowne akt Dawnych* (Zespol 437, Sygnatura 30). Warsaw, Poland. Microfilm image obtained from Brian J. Lenius of the birth of Apolonia Wild, 12-Nov-1863.

[16] Muzylowice Roman Catholic Parish. *Liber Natorum 1845-1887.* p.112, 1866-20. Microfilm GSU_2380055, item 1. *Archiwum Glowne akt Dawnych* (Zespol 437, Sygnatura 30). Warsaw, Poland. Microfilm image obtained from Brian J. Lenius of the birth of Eva Wild, 30-Aug-1866.

[17] Muzylowice Roman Catholic Parish. *Liber Natorum 1845-1887.* p.122, 1869-2. Microfilm GSU_2380055, item 1. *Archiwum Glowne akt Dawnych* (Zespol 437, Sygnatura 30). Warsaw, Poland. Microfilm image obtained from Brian J. Lenius of the birth of Thomas Wild, 02-Jan-1869.

[18] Lenius, Brian J. (compiler). *Franz Wild Siblings at the Time of his Wedding.* Table. 2017. This table of information provides details about the births, marriages, children, and immigration information for the siblings of Franz Wild who were alive at the time of his wedding. Several sources of records for the Roman Catholic parish of Muzylowice held in the Lenius library collection were used to compile this table (Appendix XII).

[19] Schmidt, Josef. "*Bilder aus dem Leben und Treiben der Deutschen in Galizien*" (Photos from the Hustle and Bustle of the Germans from Galicia). *Kalender des Bundes der christlichen Deutschen in Galizien.* p.128. 1911. Lemberg [Austro-Hungary]. Republished on CD by Alfred Konrad. 2012. Photo obtained from Brian J. Lenius.

[20] Wilde, Kathleen. Family collection. Franz Wild photo in uniform.

[21] Olinyk, Dave. M. E-mail. 23-Nov-2017. Identification of uniform and rank for photo of Franz Wild.

[22] Olinyk, Dave. M. E-mail. 23-Nov-2017. "Common AH Badges of Rank" from Badges of Rank Austro-Hungarian Austro-Hungarian Land Forces 1848-1918 By Glenn Jewison & Jörg C. Steiner
http://www.austro-hungarian-army.co.uk/badges/badges.htm

23 Monks of Tabor, Holy Transformation Monastery, Redwood Valley, CA. Icon painting of St. John the Baptist by Fr. Damian. https://monksofmttabor.com/icons

24 Lenius, Brian J. Personal communication. E-mail. 9-Dec-2017. See also https://en.wikipedia.org/wiki/Edict_on_Idle_Institutions

25 For more information see, "Details of Muzylowice Genealogy Resources" section in Appendix II.

26 Lenius, Brian J. Personal communication. E-mail. 1-Nov-2017.

27 Wikipedia "Austrian Empire Provinces" https://en.wikipedia.org/wiki/Austria-Hungary https://en.wikipedia.org/wiki/Austria-Hungary#/media/File:Austria-Hungary_map_new.svg

28 Wikimedia Commons. Franz Joseph I; Emperor of Austria, King of Hungary, monarch of Austro-Hungarian Empire. ca. 1885

29 Galicia Coat of Arms; Austrian Empire and Austro–Hungarian Empire 1772-1918. http://www.hungarianheraldry.org/galicia-and-lodomeria/ http://www.galizien-deutsche.de/what-and-where-is-galicia/a-definition.htm

30 GaliciaPoland-Ukraine Yahoo Groups. Website. Administrative boundaries as of 1998 map: Magocsi, P. R., ed. 1998. Historical atlas of East Central Europe. University of Washington Press. Austrian Galicia province (Draft) delineation map created on 9/14/2004 copyright 2004 by Laurance Krupnak. Permission granted. https://groups.yahoo.com/neo/groups/GaliciaPoland-Ukraine/info

31 Untershütz, R. *Die deutschen Siedlungen in Galizien: Stand 1939*. Map of the German colonies in Galicia as of 1939 obtained from Dick Mann.

32 Wikimapia. Map section showing L'viv and Muzylowice. http://wikimapia.org/#lang=en&lat=49.831339&lon=23.972683&z=13&m=b&search=lviv%20

33 K.K. statistischen Zentralkommission. *Gemeindelexikon der im Reichsrate vertretenen Königreiche und Länder: Bearbeitet auf Grund der Ergebnisse der Volkszählung vom 31. Dezember 1900. Bd 12: Galizien*. 1024 pp. 1907. Wien (Vienna), Austria. Microfilm image of p.254. obtained from Brian J. Lenius.

34 Österreichisches Staatsarchiv. "Third Military Survey (1869-1887)". *MAPIRE: The Historical Map Portal*. Website. http://mapire.eu/en/

35 Lenius, Brian J. and Josef Wittmann. *Münchenthal Lenius-Wittmann Map.* 1989. Winnipeg. Section of map of the former German colony of Münchenthal (Muźyłowice Kolonia) and Muźyłowice Narodowe obtained from Brian J. Lenius showing houses 109, 116, 130, 154, 181, 189. This map was drawn by Brian J. Lenius based on extensive information from multiple interviews with Josef Wittmann, a colonist born in Muzylowice in 1907.

36 Lenius, Brian J. Personal communication. Email. 9-Dec-2017.

37 Lenius, Brian J. and Edward R. Rozylowicz. *Münchenthal Catholic Cemetery Burials: 1787 - 1905.* Obtained from "The Rozylowicz Family" website. http://www.rozylowicz.com/genealogy-lite/memorial.html

38 Muzylowice Roman Catholic Parish. *Copiae Natorum 1826-1904.* Archiwum Archidecezjalne w Przemyśl (AMP). Przemysl, Poland. no.1888-1 (Karl), 1888-31 (Thomas), 1891-13 (Karl), 1893-15 (Stanislaus). Bishop's copies transcribed by Anna and Maciej Orzechowski for births of the four children of Franz Wild and Veronica Kleczka. Transcript obtained from Brian J. Lenius.

39 Muzylowice Roman Catholic Parish. *Copiae Mortuorum 1826-1904.* Archiwum Archidecezjalne w Przemyśl (AMP). Przemysl, Poland. no. 1888-1. Bishop's copy transcribed by Anna and Maciej Orzechowski for the death of Karl Wild, 27-Jan-1888. Transcript obtained from Brian J. Lenius.

40 Muzylowice Roman Catholic Parish. *Copiae Natorum 1826-1904.* Archiwum Archidecezjalne w Przemyśl (AMP). Przemysl, Poland. no.1888-1 (Karl), 1888-31 (Thomas), 1891-13 (Karl), 1893-15 (Stanislaus). … Transcript obtained from Brian J. Lenius.

41 Ibid.

42 Ibid.

43 Wilde, Brian. Lineage charts for the Wild Family created merging Kathleen Wilde's Family Group sheets with Brian J. Lenius research.

44 CoinsHome: 1881 20 Franc Gold coin. 8 Forint / 20 Franc Austria-Hungary (1867-1918) Gold Franz Joseph. www.coinshome.net

45 Wikimedia Commons, 20 Kronen banknote from Austria-Hungary. https://commons.wikimedia.org/wiki/File:BanknoteA-H.jpg https://en.wikipedia.org/wiki/Austria-Hungary

46 Lenius, Brian J. Personal communication. Email. 9-Nov-2017.

47 Hobbs, Karen. "Recruiting Rules of The Austrian Army." *East European Genealogist.* Vol. 11, No. 2 (Winter 2002). pp. 6-24. Information provided by Brian J. Lenius.

48 Lenius, Brian J. Personal communication. Email. 9-Nov-2017.

49 Muzylowice Roman Catholic Parish. *Copiae Mortuorum 1826-1904.* no.1892-22. *Archiwum Archidecezjalne* w Przemyśl (AMP). Przemysl, Poland. Bishop's copy transcribed by Anna and Maciej Orzechowski for the death of Franz Wild, 01-Dec-1892. Transcript obtained from Brian J. Lenius.

50 Lenius, Brian J. Personal communication. Email. 2-Nov-2017.

51 <u>Canadian Museum of Civilization:</u> The last best west: Advertising for immigrants to western Canada, 1870–1930, National Archives of Canada File No. C-30620, June 16, 2010, (Accessed August 19, 2011). https://en.wikipedia.org/wiki/Last_Best_West

52 Library and Archives Canada. from "Moving here Staying Here. The Canadian Immigrant Experience."

53 Library and Archives Canada. from "Moving here Staying Here. The Canadian Immigrant Experience." Acc. No. 1990-119-1.

54 Library and Archives Canada. Canada, Dept. of the Interior, Annual Report, 1897, part iv, p. 15

55 Library and Archives Canada. Canada, Dept. of the Interior, Annual Report, 1897, part iv, p. 14

56 Library and Archives Canada. Poster in German for 160 free acres. C-088625 University of Winnipeg website page for "German-Canadian Studies". https://www.uwinnipeg.ca/german-canadian/index.html# . This poster is held in GARDD, RG 76 Immigration Branch Records, Vole 225, file no. 113228, part 9

57 Library and Archives Canada. Free farms for the million. ca 1893 . The Canadian West. Exhibition.

58 wethefalcons.weebly.com Topic 4: Immigration He was mainly interested in Ukraine, Galicia, Hungary, Germany .... because the residents were familiar with farming.

59 Ibid.

60 Historic Canada: Postal System, Canadian Encyclopedia. Also, History, Village of Neudorf and Prairie-Towns.com: Images, Neudorf.

61 Willis, John; Amyot Chantel, Country Post, Rural Postal Service in Canada, 1880 to 1945. Canadian Museum of Civilization, Jan 1, 2003.

62 CanadianPostageStamps.ca Between the portraits on the stamps, the initials V.R.I. signify Victoria, Queen and Empress, and below are dates 1837 and 1897, the years of the Queen's accession and her Diamond Jubilee.

63 Shannon Dittrick Lepage. Personal communication. Email. Nov, 2017. Note: Katherine would have more children once settled in Saskatchewan.

64 Lenius, Brian J. Personal communication. Email. 2-Nov-2017.

65 Wikimedia Commons: Hamburg-Amerika Linie File:2009 10 29 Plakat HapagK.jpg

66 S.S.Arcadia Voyage of the Arcadia http://onyschuk.com/the_trip_over.html Built 1896 by Harland and Wolff at Belfast, Ireland. Also USS Arcadia (ID-1605) Wikipedia

67 S.S. Arcadia maiden voyage departing Hamburg. TheShipsList.com Arcadia 1897. Passengers: Veronika Wild age 29; children: Thomas Wild, Carl Wild, Stanislaus Wild. Origin Hamburg, destination Winnipeg MB

68 Inflation Calculator: 1897 dollars in 2015. Average inflation rate 2.84%. $100 in the year 1897 equals $2,727.66 in 2015. Extrapolating $20 = $555. http://www.in2013dollars.com/1897-dollars-in-2015

69 Courtesy National Archives and Records Administration, NARA

70 Dmytro Romanchych, *1897 Voyage of the SS Arcadia* from Early Ukrainian Settlements in Canada 1895-1900 by Vladimir J. Kaye, (Toronto: University of Toronto Press, 1964)

71 FamilySearch.org: Hamburg St. Pauli port about 1900, in Hamburg, Germany. From Tracing Immigrants Origin Emigration and Immigration.

72 Ancestry.com Staatsarchiv Hamburg, Deutschland Hamburg Passenger List, 1850-1934. (database on-line. Provo, UT. Family History Center, Later Day Saints (LDS) Reading PA

73 Ibid.

74 Kaufman, Jeannie, Ancestry magazine 2009

75 Library and Archives Canada. Passenger List. SS ARCADIA arriving at Montreal, Quebec on 2 May 1897. RG76, microfilm C-4541.

76 Lenius, Brian J. Personal communication. Email. Nov-2017.

77 Isajiw and Makuch, p. 333; Swyripa, "Ukrainians", p. 1862.

78 Wiki "Ukrainian Canadians" Immigrants heading to Yorkton.

79 Doukhobors / Library and Archives Canada / C-000684 Title: "First party of Doukhobors a day's journey from Yorkton." Spring, 1889

80 Wilde, Kathleen. Family collection. The three adolescent Wild boys in field; Carl Wild, Thomas Wild, Stanley Wild

81 Wilde, Kathleen. Family collection. The Frank Golling family including the Wild boys.

82 Google Maps "Saskatchewan". Wikipedia: Lemberg, Saskatchewan.

[83] Postcard of Lemberg Saskatchewan, from the collection of Don Kaye, Prairie-Towns.com, for preservation of historical images of Western Canadian towns, http://www.prairie-towns.com/lemberg-images.html

[84] Prairie-Towns: A Railway map of Saskatchewan from about 1947. Prairie Towns.com http://prairie-towns.com/sask-map-1947.html

[85] Wilde, Kathleen. Family collection. The Wild boys grown portrait: Stanley Aloysius Wild, Carl Wild, Thomas John Wild.

[86] Wilde, Kathleen. Family Collection. The Golling Family in Saskatchewan.

[87] Lenius, Brian J. Personal communication. Email. 2-Nov-2017.

[88] Muzylowice Roman Catholic Parish. *Liber Natorum 1845-1887.* p.120b. Microfilm GSU_2380055, item 1. *Archiwum Glowne akt Dawnych* (Zespol 437, Sygnatura 30). Warsaw, Poland. Microfilm image obtained from Brian J. Lenius of a letter written from the parish in Killaly, SK to the parish in Muzylowice, 07-Jul-1937.

[89] Latin letter translated by George Plohn, authorized certified translator, Palisades, NY

[90] Muzylowice Roman Catholic Parish. *Liber Natorum 1845-1887.* p.121, 1868-16. Microfilm GSU_2380055, item 1. *Archiwum Glowne akt Dawnych* (Zespol 301, Sygnatura 30). Warsaw, Poland. Microfilm image obtained from Shannon Dittrick Lepage for the birth of Veronica Kleczko, 02-Jul-1868.

[91] Lenius, Brian J. Personal communication. Email. 2-Nov-2017.

[92] Wilde, Kathleen. Family collection. Mary Golling graduation photo from nursing school.

[93] Wilde, Kathleen. Family collection. Kate Golling graduation photo from nursing school.

[94] Wilde, Kathleen. Family collection. Veronica Golling photo in senior years.

[95] Findagrave.com "Veronica E. Kleczko Golling" St. Elizabeth Roman Catholic Church, Killaly, Saskatchewan. June Kubica Nov, 2007, Find a Grave Memorial # 22939195.

Chapter 2

[96] Daily Mail (UK), Isle of Eigg map. An ancient inscription has been found on a remote Scottish island called Eigg. Abigail Beall. Jan 23, 2917

[97] Map of Scotland designed by Lochcarron. Interactive map here: lochcarron.co.uk/clanmap/

[98] Reference the book, *Scotland Farewell the People of the Hector* by Donald MacKay *https://www.amazon.com/Scotland-Farewell-People-Donald-MacKay/dp/1896219128*

[99] Clan Donald also known as Clan MacDonald wikipedia.org. Crest of Clan MacDonald. https://en.wikipedia.org/wiki/Clan_Donald

[100] Clan Donald also known as Clan MacDonald wikipedia.org. Crest of Clan MacDonald. https://en.wikipedia.org/wiki/Clan_Donald

[101] 60 minutes. Isle of Eigg today. *60 Minutes' adventure to the Isle of Eigg.* Steve Kroft. Lisa Orlando, producer. Nov 26, 2017

[102] Ancestry.com - AncestryDNA results summary. Autosomal. Ethnicity and genetic communities. Matching Brian J. Lenius and Brian Wilde on GedMatch.com. See Appendix XI.

[103] Historical Map Acadia 1754 Wikipedia.org acadia File:Acadia_1754.png

[104] Port of Louisbourg The Canadian Encyclopedia, Military Engagements: Louisbourg, View of Louisbourg from a warship, as it would have appeared in 1744 (artwork by Lewis Parker).

[105] Arisaig, Nova Scotia, Canada map. https://arisaigns.com/

[106] St. Margaret's Church. Canadian Historic Places. iMunicipality of the County of Antigonish Heritage Property File no. 678

[107] Trunk Road, 1873 Antigonish Heritage Museum

[108] Stage Coach article, Old Train Station News, March 2014 Antigonish Heritage Museum. The Casket newsletter, *Antigonish: As Charles Dudley Warner saw it in 1873.*

[109] Ibid.

[110] "Thomas Dilworth's Spelling Book" from *Learning to Read and Write in Colonial America,* by E. Jennifer Monaghan

[111] Canada-Rail. Train Station at Antigonish. 1906

[112] Galmisdale House, with An Sgurr beyond, Isle of Eigg, late 1880's early 1890's. Wikipedia Eigg. https://en.wikipedia.org/wiki/Eigg

[113] Wilde, Brian. Lineage charts for Mary Ann MacDonald's family created by merging Kathleen Wilde's Family Group sheets with Brian J. Lenius research.

[114] Wilde, Kathleen. Family collection. John A. MacDonald family in front of house.

[115] Wilde, Kathleen. Family collection. John A. MacDonald home landscape scene, Arisaig, Nova Scotia

[116] Horse and carriage used for "Sunday" travel. Heil family, Lemberg, Saskatchewan ca. 1912

[117] Wilde, Kathleen. Family collection. Ann MacDonald as a youth, Mary Ann MacDonald's mother.

[118] Wilde, Kathleen. Family collection. Ann MacDonald as a senior, Mary Ann MacDonald's mother.

[119] Wilde, Kathleen. Family collection. Alexander (Sandy) MacDonald, Mary Ann MacDonald's eldest brother

[120] Wilde, Kathleen. Family collection. Catherine (Kay) Eileen MacDonald

[121] Ibid.

[122] Parade at Mount St. Bernard Academy c 1912. Imagine Antigonish.ca http://www.imagineantigonish.ca/the-wild-geese-the-parade-of-mount-st-bernard-academy-women-c1912/
Only on Sundays and holidays were they allowed to walk into town, two by two, under close watch of the Sisters of the Congregation of Notre Dame (CND), c 1912. Courtesy of Bart Sears, C. J. MacGillivray album & Antigonish Heritage Museum. Restoration: Anne Louise MacDonald

[123] Normal School, Truro, NS, probably 1915, Photograph, McCord Museum. Wm. Notman & Son. VIEW-8297. http://collections.musee-mccord.qc.ca/en/collection/artifacts/VIEW-8297 Creative Commons

[124] Wilde, Kathleen. Family collection. Provincial Normal School Class 1907 Truro Nova Scotia.

[125] Wilde, Kathleen. Family collection. Mary Ann MacDonald with students in Western Canada.

[126] Wilde, Kathleen. Family collection. Thomas John Wild and Mary Ann MacDonald on their wedding day.

[127] Wilde, Kathleen. Family collection. Thomas John, Mary Ann Wild with baby Kathleen Wilde on vacation at Qu'Appelle Valley.

[128]Forebears.io Wild Surname Meaning & Statistics <http://forebears.io/surnames/wild>

[129] Society of the Little Flower. Littleflower.eu St. Theresa of Lisieux with sister Celine.

[130] Wilde, Kathleen. Family collection. Wild boys in front of grain elevator.

[131] A Saskatchewan wheat field. Photos.com .The Globe and Mail Sept 13, 2011

Chapter 3

[132] Prairie-Town web site. Melville Saskatchewan. 3rd and Main Street. http://www.prairie-towns.com/melville-1.html

[133] Prairie-Town web site. Melville Saskatchewan, Municipal Hospital. http://www.prairie-towns.com/melville-72.html

[134] Folk Song Index. "It Ain't Going to Rain No More". 20 weeks on the U.S. charts. Written 1919, recorded 1923.

[135] Wikipedia.org - Barney Google with lyrics. https://en.wikipedia.org/wiki/Barney_Google_and_Snuffy_Smith

[136] Wikipedia.org Barney Google

[137] Wilde, Kathleen. Family collection. Kathleen Wilde with dogs Tricksie and Rover

[138] Arcola Sask. Lumber business hauling trees.

[139] School room typical Prairies. Historical Photos

[140] Shield of arms of Saskatchewan. Government of Saskatchewan web site, Emblems and Flags. Photo: Confederation Plaza, Victoria, Vancouver Island, British Columbia. Canadian Encyclopedia. 2013

[141] VirtualMuseum.ca Churches of South Central Saskatchewan JoeVille Catholic Church in 1922

[142] Saskatchewan Newspaper Article "Melville Pioneer Passes in Windsor" Kay Wilde Family Archives.

[143] Buchanan, Donald. Pioneering Photographers. South Saskatchewan Photo Museum. digital.scaa.sk.ca http://digital.scaa.sk.ca/gallery/PioneeringPhotography/themeframe.php?theme=Agriculture

[144] Wilde, Kathleen. Family collection. Hal Wilde military photo, Bomber Pilot RCAF.

[145] Bomber Command Museum ca. The Lancaster Avro Bomber. http://www.bombercommandmuseum.ca/lancbomber.html

[146] Ibid.

[147] Wilde, Kathleen. Family collection. Hal Wilde on leave in Scotland during WWII.

Chapter 4

[148] Saskatchewan Settlement Experience. Provincial Archives of Saskatchewan. Agriculture: Farming Operations saskarchives.com

[149] Ibid.

[150] Ibid.

[151] Wilde, Kathleen. Family collection. Photo of Killaly Saskatchewan

[152] SportsLogos.net Toronto Maple Leafs Logos used from 1928-1938.

[153] Wilde, Kathleen. Family collection John Harold Wilde with brother Ron Wilde in front of grain elevator,

[154] WikiMedia Commons. File:Caboose pulled by horses taking children to school (23309950789).jpg Provincial Archives of Alberta

[155] *Grain Elevator at La Salle Manitoba* 1931 by Walter Phillips. b1913. Woodcut. The Canadian West Exhibition. Credit: Library and Archives Canada, Acc. No. 1989-228-1 Copyright: Expired. C- 110906

[156] Buchanan, Donald. Pioneering Photographers. South Saskatchewan Photo Museum. digital.scaa.sk.ca

[157] Saskatchewan Settlement Experience. 1929 Newspaper. Provincial Archives of Saskatchewan. saskarchives.com 1920-1930 Slide Show.

[158] Saskatoon photo. Saskatoon Berry Institute. (SaskatoonBerryInstitute.org)

[159] Wilde, Kathleen. Family collection. Thomas Wild with sons in front of grain elevator in winter.

[160] Wilde, Kathleen. Family collection. Family Portrait. (l-r) Hugh Gerald Wilde, Ron Joseph Wilde, Mary Ann Wilde, Thomas John Wild, Kathleen Wilde, John Harold "Hal" Wilde and Ralph Maurice Wilde. See also Chapter 2: The Name Change: Wild to Wilde.

Appendix

[161] Rozylowicz, Edward F. Photo: Muzylowice-Münchenthal 2007. " Schnerch Family" website <http://sznerch.weebly.com/>

162 Ibid.

163 Muzhylovychi cemetery 2017 (BJL_IMG_22955).jpg b) Citation: Lenius, Brian J. Personal photo. 06-Jun-2017. Photo obtained from Brian J. Lenius showing the long view of the Münchenthal Roman Catholic Cemetery.

164 Muzhylovychi monument 2017 (BJL_IMG_22961).jpg b) Citation: Lenius, Brian J. Personal photo. 06-Jun-2017. Close-up photo obtained from Brian J. Lenius showing a close-up view of the Münchenthal German Catholic cemetery monument.

165 Muzhylovychi monument German2 panel 2017 (BJL_IMG_22971).jpg b) Citation: Lenius, Brian J. Personal photo. 06-Jun-2017. Photo obtained from Brian J. Lenius showing the black panel with the Wild and also Schnerch surnames.

166 Muzhylovychi monument Polish panel 2017 (BJL_IMG_22968).jpg b) Citation: Lenius, Brian J. Personal photo. 06-Jun-2017. Photo obtained from Brian J. Lenius showing the black panel with the Kleczko surname.

167 Rozylowicz, Edward F. and Brian J. Lenius. Black panel message on the Münchenthal cemetery monument. English language. 8-Jul-2008. "Rozylowicz Family" website <http://www.rozylowicz.com/genealogy-lite/memorial.html>. Image obtained from Brian J. Lenius.

168 Archival photo of the Visitation of Our Blessed Mary Church. Date: Unknown. Lenius, Brian J. Personal photo.

169 Munchenthal RC Church 2017-08-21 (BJL_IMG_24483).jpg b) Citation: Lenius, Brian J. Personal photo. 21-Aug-2017. Photo obtained from Brian J. Lenius of ruined Münchenthal Roman Catholic Church.

170 Hoedel, Simone: Mariahilf Roman Catholic Cemetery. Separate from Saint Elizabeth Roman Catholic Cemetery. Killaly, Saskatchewan. Find a Grave. Photo: June Kubica. Hoedel, Simone. "Early Settlers to Mariahilf, Saskatchewan, 1900 - 2 (republished with transcribed text)" http://simonehoedelfamilyhistory.blogspot.com/2018/01/early-settlers-to-mariahilf_3.html

171 Hoedel, Simone and Thiele, William: History of St. Elizabeth Roman Catholic Parish in Killaly SK. http://simonehoedelfamilyhistory.blogspot.com/2018/01/st-elizabeth-parish-history-from-willy.html and
 http://reocities.com/Heartland/Valley/3203/

172 Ancestry.com - AncestryDNA results summary. Autosomal. Ethnicity and genetic communities.

173 Lenius, Brian J. and Wilde, Brian: 4th Cousins Lineage Matching Chart. Genetic Genealogy: GedMatch.com

[174] Lenius, Brian J. Personal communication. Email. Nov 29, 2017. Research on Franz Wild's family at the time of his wedding. Note: Marianna Lenius, married to Josef Wild, were likely in attendance at Franz Wild's wedding.

Bibliography

Jacobs, A.J.   *It's All Relative: Adventures Up and Down the World's Family Tree* 2017

Kann, Robert A.   *A History of the Hapsburg Empire 1526-1918* 1980

MacKay, Donald   *Scotland Farewell: The People of the Hector* 2006

MacLean, Raymond   *History of Antigonish* Casket Printing 1976

Serhil, Plokhy   *The Gates of Europe: A History of Ukraine* 2015

Library and Archives Canada. *Moving Here Staying Here. The Canadian Immigrant Experience.*